Frédéric Bastiat, Edward Robert Pearce

Popular fallacies regarding trade and foreign duties

Frédéric Bastiat, Edward Robert Pearce

Popular fallacies regarding trade and foreign duties

ISBN/EAN: 9783337130930

Printed in Europe, USA, Canada, Australia, Japan

Cover: Foto ©Suzi / pixelio.de

More available books at **www.hansebooks.com**

POPULAR FALLACIES

REGARDING

TRADE AND FOREIGN DUTIES:

BEING THE

"*SOPHISMES ÉCONOMIQUES*"

OF

FRÉDÉRIC BASTIAT,

*Late Member of the Institute
of France.*

ADAPTED TO THE PRESENT TIME

BY

EDWARD ROBERT PEARCE.

CASSELL, PETTER, GALPIN & CO.:

LONDON, PARIS & NEW YORK.

1882.

PREFACE.

No work with which I am acquainted puts the *principles* of Free Trade more forcibly—by means of the most homely illustrations—than the "Sophismes Économiques" of Bastiat. The importance of being armed with principles cannot be over-estimated; they are a touchstone which should be ever at hand to test and explain the changing conditions of home and foreign trade. While figures change from day to day, principles remain unchanged.

In the following pages I have been able to reduce the "Sophismes" to nearly half their original size, the present phase of the controversy rendering much that was first written unnecessary. I have given the illustrations an English form, by changing francs to pounds, French names to English, &c., and a few illustrations which were somewhat out cf date I have altered to suit the present time. Some new passages which have been introduced are included within brackets [ ]. I have made use of the English edition brought out in 1846 by the late Mr. Porter, the well-known author of the "Progress of the Nation."

E. R. P.

London,
January 10th, 1882.

CONTENTS.

—◆—

POPULAR FALLACIES

REGARDING

TRADE AND FOREIGN DUTIES.

—◦◦◦—

CHAPTER I.

FREE TRADE—FAIR TRADE.

[A LEAGUE has been formed " for the preservation of our home industries and the protection of our national labour against unfair foreign competition." The manifesto from which these words are taken goes on to say, " The policy of one-sided trade which has so long been maintained in this country is enabling foreigners to gain the monopoly of our markets, to displace British labour, and to deprive British workmen of their purchasing power—*i.e.*, of their wages."

The members of this League—who, though they use the word Protection, object to be called " Protectionists," preferring to be known as " Fair Traders"—deny our right to use the words Free Trade as descriptive of the system of trade at present existing in this country. They say that Free Trade only exists between us and those countries which impose no taxes upon our productions—that ours is only a free importation system, a one-sided Free Trade, for foreign countries tax our productions while we do not tax theirs, and that from this one-sided system we are suffering loss. " Isolated Free Trade," says the manifesto already mentioned, " is ruining the country."

The Fair Trade manifesto further says that " foreign nations do not tax their consumers by taxing British commodities ;" from which we are meant to infer that if we taxed foreign commodities we should not be taxing the British consumer.

The Fair Trade League, while anxious to protect English labour against unfair foreign competition, declare that they are convinced Free Traders, and that their object is to obtain real Free Trade—viz., the abolition of the taxes levied by foreign countries upon our productions. This accomplished, the League would have no objection to our levying none in return. We are to bring this about by marshalling ourselves under the banner of reciprocity and "holding out threats of retaliatory measures, which, if necessary, are to be strictly enforced." I do not know whether any one seriously believes that our return to Protection would cause foreign countries to adopt Free Trade. I should have thought that if one country protecting against another country could have led to this result, the number of countries at present levying protective duties would surely have been sufficient to effect it without adding one more to the number.

The League further proposes that there should be a confederation of the mother country and the colonies, for the purpose of carrying out within the empire the principles of absolute Free Trade. Many other propositions are made in the manifesto of the League, but these are sufficient for our present purpose.

The aim of this little treatise is to show that every one of these propositions involves a fallacy—that is to say, involves and conceals assumptions on matters of fact which are entirely erroneous.

Every person must be considered in two lights—as a producer and as a consumer. The Fair Traders consider only the producer. I intend to prove that the levying of taxes upon imports, which the Fair Traders propose, would not lead to the employment of one single additional labourer or workman, nor would it raise the wages of labour one penny, while it would cause an increase in the cost of articles of consumption. As every one, without exception, is a consumer, it would be injurious to all.

The strength of the Fair Trade movement is due partly, no doubt, to selfish interest, but it rests mostly upon error—upon *incomplete truths*. Let me illustrate what I mean.

It is common enough to hear it said of the extravagance of a spendthrift that "it is all good for trade." Such root has this fallacy taken, that Mandeville has enunciated the paradox that "private vices are public benefits." The strength of this fallacy lies in its setting forth an incomplete truth; the good is visible to the external eye, the evil can only be perceived by the mind.]

The clumsy son of your excellent grocer breaks the large pane of glass in his father's shop. One of the spectators consoles the unfortunate grocer by saying "It is an ill-wind that blows nobody good. Everybody must live, and what would become of the glaziers if panes of glass were never broken?" This contains an entire theory. It costs £5 to repair the damage, and you therefore say it brings £5 to the glazier's trade—it encourages that trade to that amount. I grant it: you reason justly. The glazier comes, repairs the window, rubs his hands, and blesses the careless son. All this is *that which is seen.*

It is not seen that as our shopkeeper has spent £5 upon one thing he cannot spend it upon another. *It is not seen* that if he had not the window to replace he would have purchased some clothes, or books, or furniture, or taken his family for an outing, or invested the money in his trade.

The window is broken, and the glazier's trade is encouraged : *that is seen.*

Had the window not been broken, the tailor's trade (or some other) would have been encouraged to the ·amount of £5 : this is *that which is not seen.*

The sum total, then, of industry *in general,* of *national labour,* is not affected whether windows are broken or not ; but how about the grocer? He has spent £5 upon the window, and has no more for his money than he had before ; only he is poorer by £5. Had the window not been broken, he would have had the enjoyment of some more clothes or something else, and the window too.

Now, as the grocer is part of society, we must come to the conclusion that in making an estimate of its labours and enjoyments it has lost the value of the broken window.

[We shall presently see that if we adopt the retaliatory measures recommended by the Fair Traders, we shall simply transfer a certain amount of labour from the tailor or the bookseller to the glazier ; the community, as represented by the grocer, being the poorer by that amount.]

CHAPTER II.

ABUNDANCE—SCARCITY.

WHICH is better—abundance or scarcity?

"What!" you will exclaim, "how can this be made a question? Is it possible to maintain that scarcity is the foundation of the well-being of men?" Yes, this has been maintained; it is maintained every day, and I do not hesitate to say that the *theory of scarcity* is extremely popular. It is advanced in conversation, in newspapers, in books, in Parliament; and although the assertion may appear extravagant, it is nevertheless true that political economy will have fulfilled its task when it shall have caused the simple proposition—that riches consist in the abundance of things—to be universally accepted.

But recently the cry was, "We are suffering from overproduction." Therefore abundance is dreaded.

We now hear every day, "The foreigner is flooding our markets with his goods." Therefore we fear abundance.

Have not some said, "Let bread be dear, and agricultural depression will disappear"? But bread can only be dear because it is scarce, therefore these men extol scarcity.

How does it happen that abundance appears to be dreaded, and scarcity to be desired? I intend to trace this illusion to its source.

It is seen that a man becomes rich in proportion as he draws a greater profit from his work—that is to say, according as he sells at a higher price. He sells at a higher price, in proportion to the rarity—the scarcity—of the kind of product which is the object of his industry. Hence it is concluded that, with regard to him at least, scarcity enriches him. Applying successively this reasoning to all manufacturers and producers, *the theory of scarcity* is deduced. Hence we pass to the application; and, in order to favour all classes of producers, dearness is to be artificially excited, the scarcity of everything is to be brought about by prohibition and restriction.

The same reasoning may be pursued in the case of abundance. It is observed that when any particular produce abounds, it is sold at a low price ; then the producer gains less. If all producers are in the same situation, they are all miserable ; it is then abundance which ruins society. Accordingly, men seek by legislation to oppose abundance.

This fallacy obtains all its force from being applied, not to all producers generally, but now to this branch of industry, now to that. It is a syllogism ; not *false*, but *incomplete*. But whatever there may be which is *true* in a syllogism is always and necessarily present to the mind. On the other hand, *incompleteness* is a negative quality, an absent *datum* which it is very possible, and even very easy, to hold of no account.

Man produces in order to consume. He is, at the same time, a producer and a consumer. The reasoning which I have just established considers him only as a producer. Consider him as a consumer, and we arrive at an opposite conclusion. Might it not in truth be said :—

The cheaper he buys the richer is the consumer. Things are bought cheap in proportion to their abundance ; then abundance enriches him : and this reasoning extended to all consumers would conduct to the *theory of abundance !*

It is the imperfectly comprehended notion of *exchange* which produces these illusions. Sellers desire a dear market, buyers a cheap market.

If man were a solitary animal, if he worked exclusively for himself, if he consumed directly the fruit of his own labour—in a word, if he did not *exchange*, then the theory of scarcity would never have been introduced into the world. It would be too evident that abundance would be advantageous to him, in whatever way it might come to him ; whether it were the result of his industry, of ingenious tools, of powerful machinery which he might have invented, or whether he owed it to the fertility of the soil, to the liberality of nature, or even to a mysterious *invasion* of productions which the waves might have brought from other parts and abandoned to his use on the shore. The solitary man, in order to insure a demand for his own labour, would never dream of breaking the instruments which spared it, of neutralising the fertility of the soil, of restoring to the sea the goods which it had borne to him. He would easily comprehend that labour is not an end, but a means ; that it would be absurd to reject the end for fear of injuring the means. He would comprehend that *the economy of labour* is another name for *progress*.

But *exchange* confuses our view of this simple truth.   In civilised life, with the separation of occupations which it brings about, the production and consumption of an article are not combined in the same individual.   Each is therefore induced to see in his own labour no longer a means but an end. Exchange creates relatively to each article two opposing interests—that of the producer and that of the consumer.

Let us take a producer of any description; what is his interest?   It consists in these two things: 1st, That the smallest possible number of persons should occupy themselves in the same business as himself; 2nd, That the greatest possible number should seek for the produce of this kind of labour—competition limited and sale unlimited.

What is the interest of the consumer?   A large supply and a small demand.

One of these two interests must necessarily coincide with the social or general interest, and the other be contrary to it.

But which of these should legislation favour as being the expression of the public good, if indeed it ought to favour either?

In order to arrive at this knowledge, it is sufficient to inquire what would happen if the Legislature were to seek to realise the secret desires of manufacturers and producers.

In the character of producers, it must be allowed each of us has anti-social wishes.   Are we wool growers?   Should we be grieved if there were a murrain affecting all the sheep in the world except ours?   *This is the theory of scarcity.*   Are we proprietors of iron-works?   We should desire that there was no other iron in the market than that which we brought there, however much the public might be in want of it; and precisely because this want was so urgently felt and so imperfectly satisfied, we should receive a high price for our own iron.   *This is, again, the theory of scarcity.*   Are we farmers? We say let bread be dear—that is to say, scarce—and the agriculturist will flourish.   *This is still the theory of scarcity.*

Do we manufacture silk goods?   We desire to sell them at the most advantageous price *for us*.   We would willingly consent to the prohibition of all rival manufactures; and if we dare not attempt its realisation, nor even publicly express a wish to do so, we still would endeavour to bring it about by indirect means; for example, by excluding foreign silks, in order to diminish the *quantity in the market*, and so produce a scarcity.

We could thus pass under review every branch of industry, and should always find that producers, in so far as they are such, have anti-social views.   It follows thence, that if the secret wishes of each producer were realised, the world would rapidly retrograde towards barbarism.   The sail would proscribe steam, the oar would proscribe the sail, the railway would have to cede the right of transit to the cart, this again to the horse, and the horse to the pedlar.

But if we proceed to consider the immediate interest of the consumer, we shall find that it is in perfect harmony with the general interest—with what the well-being of the human race demands.

When the buyer presents himself in the market, he desires to find it abundantly provided.   That the seasons may be propitious to the gathering in of agricultural produce ; that inventions more and more admirable may place within his reach a greater number of articles of necessity and of comfort ; that time and labour may be saved ; that distances may vanish ; that the spirit of peace and of justice may allow a diminution in the weight of taxes ; that barriers of every kind may fall—in all this the interest of the consumer runs parallel with the public interest.   He can push his secret wishes to the very extreme, without his wishes ceasing to be philanthropic.

I supposed just now a Legislature composed of manufacturers and producers, of which each member would frame as a law his secret wish in the character of producer ; and I said that a code emanating from this assembly would be systematised monopoly—the theory of scarcity put in practice.

In the same way, a chamber where each would consult his own interest as consumer would end by systematising liberty, the abolition of all restrictive measures, the overturning of all artificial barriers ; in a word, by the realisation of the theory of abundance.

It follows thence :

That to consult exclusively the immediate interest of production, is to consult an anti-social interest.

That to consult exclusively the immediate interest of consumption, is to consult the general interest.

As a radical antagonism exists between the seller and the buyer, the producers seek to make the laws, which ought to be at least neutral, take the part of the seller against the buyer, of the producer against the consumer—of dearness against cheapness, of scarcity against abundance.

Now I ask, would the people be better nourished under such laws, because there was *less* bread, meat, and sugar in the country? Would they be better clothed because there was *less* wool, linen, and cloth?

But it is said, if the foreigner *inundates* us with his produce, he will carry away all our money.

We shall see later on if this be so.

[Before the Fair Traders brought forward their proposals for retaliatory duties, "over-production" was pointed to as the especial cause of the prevailing commercial depression. A diminution of production as a remedy was popular with both masters and men. It is plausible, but short-sighted. The natural remedy for a too limited market is extension, by cheapening the article produced; the artificial remedy is to render it dearer. A lower price extends old markets, and opens new. Every idle day, every holiday, means non-creation of wealth, and every article produced is wanted to exchange. If the cotton spinners are right in reducing production, the collier is right in producing less coal, the farmer in producing less food, and so on. Every producer will have created less exchangeable wealth, will get more for the *one* thing he sells, and give more for the *twenty* he buys. To the workman this is especially injurious, for whereas the capitalist can store up his capital, the labourer cannot store up his labour; if he does not sell it day by day it is lost.

But the theory of "over-production"—one form of the theory of scarcity—has now been dropped, to give place to another form of the same theory—viz., restrictions on the importations of foreign produce.

It may be well to be reminded here of the following causes of disturbance to trade and manufactures, all of which falling within the past ten years, many deem alone sufficient to account for the state of commercial depression from which the country has been suffering.

At the beginning of the decade we had the Franco-German war disturbing the industry of those countries, and causing a large expenditure in England. Following upon this came the railway mania in the United States, during which iron rails rose to £20 a ton * (1873), to fall within four years to the other extreme—viz., £4 10s. a ton. From 1870 to 1874 foreign countries were borrowing from us at the rate of nearly £100,000,000 a year. These immense loans went abroad, not in the form of money, but as materials for railways, telegraphs, gas-works, water-works, tramways, as steam coal, fire-arms, machinery, &c. That is to say, the money was spent upon English labour, and the products of that labour were exported. We know that this must have been the case from the returns of bullion, which show that in each of those years we imported more gold and silver than we exported (p. 40). Next came repudiation of their debts by foreign borrowers, and we found ourselves in the possession of worthless bonds to the value of £1,000,000,000. Not only did the interest—some £60,000,000 annually—cease, but the unpleasant experience diminished loans to foreigners ; and as these loans had all gone abroad in the form of English labour, the employment of English labour suffered a severe check. Besides this, China and India have both suffered from famine, and consequently the spending power of those two countries was for a time diminished. Since the Franco-German war larger standing armies than before have been maintained in Europe, and the spending power of the countries which have maintained them has been thereby lessened. Trade has been disturbed by a considerable rise in the value of gold, owing mainly to the fact that Germany has made it her standard metal, and that the United States and Italy have both returned to specie payments after using paper money for many years. Added to all this, we have suffered from three unusually bad harvests in this country. Are not these things sufficient to explain the commercial depression which has existed, without seeking to lessen production or to impugn the Free Trade principles which we have adopted ?]

* Many private firms were converted into joint-stock companies at the then inflated prices, and the directors from time to time complain that they are unable to declare any dividends.

CHAPTER III.

OBSTACLE—OBJECT.

MAN is, by nature, entirely destitute of appliances. Between his state of destitution and the satisfying of his wants there exists a multitude of *obstacles*, which it is the end of labour to surmount. It is curious to investigate how and why these *obstacles* to his well-being have themselves become in his eyes the *cause* of his well-being.

I require to transport myself a thousand miles. But between the points of departure and arrival, mountains, sea, rivers, morasses, forests—in a word, *obstacles* interpose ; and to vanquish these obstacles I must use many efforts, or, what is the same thing, I must cause others to use many efforts, and for these I must pay them. It is clear with regard to this case that I should have been in a better condition if these obstacles had not existed.

In the journey through life, man requires to assimilate to himself a prodigious quantity of nourishment, to guard himself against the inclemencies of the seasons, and to preserve himself against and relieve himself from a crowd of evils. Hunger, thirst, sickness, heat, cold, are so many obstacles set up on his path.

In a state of isolation he must combat them all by hunting, fishing, farming, spinning, weaving, building ; and it is clear that it would be better for him that these obstacles existed in a less degree, and still better if they did not exist at all. In society he does not attack personally each of these many obstacles, but others do it for him ; and in return he removes one of the obstacles by which his fellow-creatures are surrounded.

It is clear also that, considering things in the mass, it is much better for men taken together—for society—that the obstacles be as weak and also as few as possible.

But if we investigate the views of men as they have been modified by exchange, it will soon be perceived how they have happened to confound wants with wealth, and the obstacle with the object.

The separation of occupations causes each man, instead of striving on his own account with all the obstacles which surround him, to combat only with one ; to combat it, not for himself alone, but for the benefit of his fellow men, who in their turn render him a similar service.

But it results from this that each man sees the immediate cause of his riches in the obstacle which he has made it his profession to combat upon account of others. The greater this obstacle, the more disposed his fellow men are to remunerate him for having vanquished it; that is to say, the more disposed are they to labour to remove, for his benefit, those obstacles which inconvenience and trouble him.

A physician, for example, does not occupy himself in baking his bread, in constructing his instruments, in weaving or making up his clothes. Others do these things for him, and in return he combats the maladies which afflict his patients. The more numerous, intense, and frequent these maladies are, the more willing others are—the more they are forced, indeed —to work for his personal advantage. In this point of view, illness—that is to say, a general obstacle to the well-being of men—promotes the well-being of an individual. All producers, in what concerns them, reason in the same manner. The shipowner draws his profits from the obstacle called *distance;* the farmer from that which is called *hunger;* the manufacturer of stuffs from that called *cold;* the instructor lives upon *ignorance;* the physician upon the *maladies* of men. It is thus quite true that each profession has an immediate interest in the continuation, and even in the aggravation, of the special obstacle which forms the object of its exertions.

Seeing this, theorists who base their system upon these individual opinions arrive at the following conclusions : They say, what we require is wealth; labour is wealth. To multiply obstacles is to give an incitement to industry.

If we prevent the bringing of sugar from where it is cheaply produced, we create an obstacle to our procuring it. A certain number of our citizens will set themselves to contend against this obstacle, and will thereby make their fortunes.

Here, it will be said, are certain men who want casks for their beer. It is an obstacle; and here are certain other men who employ themselves in removing this obstacle by making casks. Suppose an ingenious machine is invented, which cuts down the oak, squares it, divides it into a number of staves, puts them together, and transforms them into beer barrels. The obstacle is very much diminished, and with it the fortune of the coopers.

Maintain them both by a law. Prohibit the machine. Toil then —the primeval curse of man—is a blessing.

In order to penetrate to the bottom of this fallacy, it is sufficient to say that human labour is not an *end* but a *means*. It is never left without employment. If one obstacle fails, it will attack another, and humanity is freed from two obstacles by the same amount of labour which would have destroyed but one only. If the art of the coopers ever became useless, their labour would take another direction. But from what fund, it may be asked, would they be remunerated ? Precisely from that which remunerates them now; for when a mass of labour becomes disposable through the removal of an obstacle, a corresponding amount of remuneration becomes disposable also.

CHAPTER IV.

EFFORT—RESULT.

WE have just seen that between the arising of our wants and their being satisfied obstacles are interposed. By the efforts of industry we surmount these obstacles.

But by what is our well-being, our wealth, measured ? Is it by the result of effort, or by the effort itself? There must always exist a relation between the effort employed and the result obtained. Does progress consist in the relative increase of the second or of the first term of this relation?

According to the first system, wealth is the result of labour. It increases in proportion to the increase of the relation of the result to the effort. Absolute perfection consists in the infinite separation of the two terms—that is to say, effort nothing, result infinite.

According to the second system, the effort itself constitutes and measures wealth. To progress is to increase the ratio of the effort to the result.

The first system naturally welcomes everything which tends to diminish work and to increase its results : powerful machines, which add to the efficiency of man's labour ; exchange, which allows of our deriving the greatest benefit from natural agents distributed in divers degrees upon the surface of the globe ;

intelligence which makes discoveries ; experience which veri-
fies ; competition which stimulates, &c.

Logically, also, it follows that, to fulfil the conditions of the
second system, everything which has the effect of increasing
work and diminishing its result must be desired—prohibitions,
privileges, monopolies, abolition of machinery, sterility, &c.

It is well to remark, that the *universal practice* of men is
always directed by the principle of the first doctrine. A man
has never been seen, and never will be seen—be he farmer,
manufacturer, merchant, artisan, soldier, author, or *savant*—who
does not concentrate all the powers of his mind upon the
effort to make better, to make more quickly, to make more
economically—in a word, *to make more with less.*

The opposite doctrine is in use by theorists, who nevertheless, in what concerns them personally, act as everybody
else does—to obtain from labour the greatest possible sum of
useful effects. This is always so when we set out on a false
principle. It soon brings results so absurd and so mischievous,
that we are forced to check ourselves. The punishment would
follow too soon upon the error, and expose it at once. But
in matters of speculative industry, such as these theorists
reason upon, a false principle may be followed a long time
before they are warned of its falseness by the complicated
consequences to which it leads ; and when at length these
consequences are revealed, they act according to the opposite
principle, contradict themselves, and seek to justify their change
of front by asserting that in political economy there is no
absolute principle. Let us, then, see if these two opposite
principles do not reign by turns.

The farmer who desires a tax on foreign wheat lends all his
efforts to this double end. As a farmer, his aim is to save
labour and produce wheat as cheaply as possible, for the cheaper
his product the greater is the remuneration he receives. When
he prefers a good plough to a bad one, improves his land,
and calls to his aid all the processes which science and
experience have revealed to him, he has, and he can have,
but one end—*to diminish the ratio of the effort to the result.*
We have not, indeed, any other means of recognising the skill
of the cultivator and the perfection of a process but by ascer-
taining what these have retrenched from the effort and added
to the result ; and as all the farmers in the world act upon this
principle, we may say that the whole human race, without
doubt for its own advantage, endeavours to obtain everything,

whether it be bread or any other production, as cheap as possible, that is to say, with the least amount of labour.

This tendency once admitted, should indicate to us in what manner we ought to second industry; for it is absurd to say that the laws of men ought to operate in an inverse direction to the laws—for we may call such tendency a law—of Providence.

But when the farmer, as a politician and a voter, says, " I comprehend nothing of the theory of cheapness; I prefer rather to see bread dearer and work more abundant ;" it is very evident that the principle of the farmer as a politician and a voter is diametrically opposed to that of the farmer as a farmer   To be consistent with himself, he should vote against all restriction ; or he should carry out on his farm the principle that he follows out at the ballot box. We should then see him sowing his seed on the most barren land, for he would succeed thus in *working much* to *obtain little.* We should see him banish the plough, since the culture with the spade would gratify his double wish—bread dearer, and work more abundant.

Restriction has for its avowed end, and for its recognised effect, to increase labour. It has also for its avowed end, and for its recognised effect, to promote dearness, which is nothing else than the scarcity of products—*labour infinite, produce nothing.*

One often hears it said that " labour constitutes the riches of a people." This is true if it mean that the results of labour constitute the riches of the people ; but not true if it mean (as it does) that the intensity of labour is the measure of the riches. Put restrictive duties, it is said, upon foreign produce, double the work for a specified article, and you double the riches; thence riches are measured not by the result but by the intensity of labour. Accordingly, if a country is in a critical situation, it is because she has produced too much, her labour has been too fruitful; her people too well fed, too well clothed, too well provided with everything; too rapid production has outstripped their desires. An end must then be put to this scourge, and in order to do this they must be forced by restrictions to work more and to produce less. We ought to desire that human intelligence should grow weak and become extinguished ; for as long as it exists, it will incessantly strive to augment the ratio of the end to the means, and of the product to the work ; for it is therein, precisely and exclusively, that intelligence consists.

CHAPTER V.

TO EQUALISE THE CONDITIONS OF PRODUCTION.

[As to our manufactures, we have been assured by Sir H. Giffard that "ever since the English ports have been open free to other people, while theirs have been closed to us, the manufactures of the country have declined."* As to agricultural produce, Sir J. Holker has told us that we are pursuing " a Quixotic policy of Free Trade, regardless of any consideration of reciprocal dealing, and that we should prevent a ruinous competition in beef, mutton, and crops."† Mr. Ecroyd says that " we must remove the food-growing trade from the United States by a small differential duty." Many others tell us that " we ought to put a tax upon foreign produce equal to the difference in cost between an article made by us and a similar article made by foreigners—that this is to insure free competition, for free competition cannot exist except there be equality of conditions and of cost."]

When a handicap race is to be run, the weight that each of the horses has to carry is proportioned to his power, and thus conditions are equalised. Applying this idea to commerce, the Fair Traders think it most desirable that the conditions of production should be equalised.

As this argument constantly recurs, I propose to examine it with care, and in doing so I entreat the attention and the patience of the reader. I will first consider the inequalities which depend upon natural causes, and afterwards those which arise out of divers conditions of taxation.

Here, as elsewhere, we again find that the theorists who favour retaliatory duties take only the point of view of the producers; while we advocate the cause of the unhappy consumers, of whom they absolutely refuse to take any account. They compare the field of industry to a handicap race, forgetting that in a handicap the race is at the same time *the means* and *the end*. The public takes no interest in the contest beyond the contest itself. But when you start your horses for the sole *end* of knowing which is the best racer, you do not weight them differently.

* At Launceston, Oct. 27, 1881. *Western Morning News.*
† At Preston, Nov. 7, 1881. *Times.*

If you have for your object the speedy arrival at the goal of important and pressing news, would you, without inconsistency, create obstacles against those horses which offered you the best conditions for speed? This is, however, what you would do in regard to industry. You forget the result sought for, which is *well-being*—which is not increased by placing obstacles in the way of its attainment.

But since we cannot bring our adversaries to our point of view, let us place ourselves in theirs, and examine the question with regard to production.

I shall seek to establish :

1st. That to bring to the same level the conditions of labour is to attack exchange in its principle.

2nd. That it is not true that the labour of a country may be destroyed by the competition of more favoured countries.

3rd. That were this even correct, retaliatory duties would not equalise the conditions of production.

4th. That Free Trade brings these conditions as much as possible to the same level.

5th. Lastly, That the least favoured countries gain the most by exchanges.

1st. To bring the conditions of labour to the same level, not only deranges markets, but attacks exchange in its principle; for all commerce is founded precisely on that diversity, or, if it be preferred, upon those inequalities of fertility, of aptitude, of climate, of temperature, which you would efface. If Devonshire sends cider to Kent, and Kent hops to Devonshire, it is because these two counties are placed in different conditions of production. Is there, then, another law for international exchanges?

2nd. It is not true, *in fact*, that the inequality of conditions between two similar branches of industry necessarily involves the destruction of that which is the least advantageously circumstanced. On the turf, when one of the horses gains the prize the others lose it ; but when two horses work for the production of what is useful, each produces in proportion to its power, and though the strongest does the most service, it does not follow that the weaker does no good at all. Wheat is grown in all the counties of England, though there are enormous differences of fertility in them ; and if by chance there is one which does not cultivate it, the reason is because its cultivation is not found profitable there. In the same manner, analogy would teach us that, under the system of Free Trade, wheat would be grown in all the kingdoms of Europe, and if there were one which renounced its growth it would be because, pursuing *its own interest*, it would have found how to make a better use of its land, of its capital, and of its labour power. And why does not the fertility of one country paralyze the agriculture of a neighbouring but less favoured country? Because, though your field produces three times more than mine, it has cost you ten times more, therefore I can still compete with you. This is all the mystery. And remark, that superiority in some respects leads to inferiority in others. It is precisely because your soil is more fertile that it is dearer : in this manner it is not *accidentally* but *necessarily* that an equilibrium, or a tendency to it, is established ; and can any one deny that Free Trade is the system which favours this tendency most ?

I have given as an example a branch of agriculture, but I could equally well have furnished an example in another branch of industry. There are tailors at Newcastle, but that does not prevent there being tailors in London, though the latter pay much more for their rent, furniture, journeymen, and living. But they have also a different class of customers, and that suffices not only to re-establish the balance but even to make it decline on their side.

When, then, we speak of equalising the conditions of labour, we must at least examine whether Free Trade does not do that which we are urged to seek from arbitrary measures.

There are two countries, A and B. A possesses all kinds of advantages over B. You, my Fair Trade opponent, immediately conclude that labour is concentrated in A, and that B is powerless, and can do nothing. A, you say, sells much more than it buys ; B buys more than it sells. I should be able to contest this point, perhaps, but I will meet you on your own ground.

By the hypothesis, labour is in great demand in A, and in consequence it soon rises in price.

Iron, coal, land, provisions, capital, are in great demand ; and they soon rise in price.

During this time labour, iron, coal, land, provisions—all are quite neglected in B, and soon everything there falls in price.

This is not all. A always selling, B always buying, money passes from B into A. It abounds in A—it is scarce in B. But abundance of money is the same as saying that it requires

much to buy all other things.   Then in A, to the real *dearness*
which arises from a very active demand, there is added a
nominal dearness consequent on the extra proportion of the
precious metals.

Scarcity of money signifies that there may be very little
expended in each purchase.   Then in B *nominal cheapness* is
combined with real *cheapness*.

Under these circumstances, industry will have all sorts of
motives, of motives, if I may so say, carried to the fourth
power, to desert A and establish itself in B.

But to return to the region of reality : we must say that it
will not have waited for this moment, as these sudden dis-
placements are repugnant to the nature of industry, and that,
from the beginning, under a system of Free Trade, it would be
progressively divided and distributed between A and B, according to the laws of supply and demand—that is to say, according
to the laws of justice and utility.

And when I say that if it were possible that industry could
be concentrated on one point, there would rise within itself,
and by its own movement, an irresistible power of *decentralisa-
tion*, I do not put forth an empty hypothesis.

[Let us listen to what the manifesto of the Fair Traders
says : " Capitalists are closing their works in England, and are
leaving the country to erect new works in Protectionist countries."   Again, " The free importation of products of labour
manufactured abroad is diminishing the home demand to such
an extent that capitalists are beginning to close their works in
this country and to erect similar works abroad, where their
capital is protected from unfair competition."   Now listen to
what a manufacturer said in the Chamber of Commerce in
Manchester, in 1842, when Protection ruled (I suppress the
figures on which he rested his demonstration) :—" Formerly
we exported cotton stuffs ; this exportation has given place to
that of yarn, which is the material for making the stuffs ; afterwards to that of machines, which are the instruments of production of the yarn ; later still, to that of capital, with which we
constructed our machines ; and lastly, to that of our workmen,
and of our industrial genius, which are the sources of our
capital.   All these elements of labour have been, the one after
the other, exercised wherever it was found that most advantage
could be made of them, where living is less dear, life more
easy ; and immense manufactories founded by English capital,

carried on by English workmen, and directed by English engineers, may be seen in the present day in Prussia, in Austria, in Saxony, in Switzerland, and in Italy."

The manifesto says nothing about agricultural depression ; I presume because it was considered patent to all. But let us hear a farmer's petition, drawn up in 1831, when Protection was doing its utmost for agriculture : " We, the gentry, magistrates, clergy, freeholders and occupiers of land in the district of the once opulent vale of Taunton, most humbly represent to your Honourable House that the cruel distress throughout the district in which we reside has arrived at an unparalleled height, and is daily increasing to an alarming extent, with a progressive decline in the value of all productions of the earth, accompanied by an overwhelming burden of taxation such as was never endured by any country, and has swallowed up the capital of the farmer, and brought the greater proportion of independent yeomen to the brink of ruin, which, without the most speedy relief, must terminate in the annihilation of this most excellent and invaluable body of men."]

You see that nature, or rather Providence, more ingenious, more wise, more foreseeing, than your narrow and rigid theorist imagines, has not willed this concentration of labour, this monopoly of every superiority, about which you argue as an absolute and irremediable fact. It has provided, by means as simple as infallible, the prevention of this by dispersion, diffusion, association, simultaneous progress—everything which your restrictive laws would paralyze as much as possible : for their tendency in isolating people is to render the diversity of their conditions much more marked, to prevent the process of levelling, to hinder their fusion, to neutralise the counterpoise, and to shut up the people in their respective superiority or inferiority.

3rd. In the third place, to say that by a retaliatory duty the conditions of production are equalised, is to use an incorrect expression which conveys error. It is not true that an import duty equalises the conditions of production. These remain after the duty the same as they were before. What the duty equalises, at most, are *the conditions of sale.* It may, perhaps, be said that I play upon words ; but I throw back the accusation upon my adversaries. It is for them to prove that production and sale are synonymous, without which proof I have a right to reproach them, if not for playing upon words, at least for confounding them.

Let me be allowed to make this point clear by an example.

Assume that the idea came into the head of some Cornish speculators to devote themselves to the production of oranges. They know that the oranges of Portugal can be sold in London for one penny each, while they, on account of the conservatories, &c., which will be necessary for their growth and preservation, on account of the cold, which is often adverse to their culture, would not be able to charge less than a shilling per orange as a remunerative price. They therefore require that the oranges of Portugal may be charged with a duty of elevenpence. By means of this duty the *conditions of production*, say they, will be equalised.

Well, I say that the *conditions of production* are not in any way changed. The law has not made Lisbon colder nor Cornwall hotter. The orange will continue to be *naturally* ripened in Portugal and *artificially* in Cornwall ; that is to say, its growth will require much more human labour in the one country than in the other. That which will be equalised are the *conditions of sale*. The Portuguese will have to sell their oranges for a shilling each, elevenpence of which will go to pay the duty. Evidently this tax will be paid by the English consumer ; and observe the whimsicality of the result. Upon each Portuguese orange consumed, the country will lose nothing, for the extra elevenpence paid for it by the consumer will go into the Treasury. There will be a displacement, but no loss. But upon each English orange consumed there will be elevenpence loss, or nearly so ; for the buyer will lose that amount most certainly, and the seller will also as certainly not gain it, since, from the hypothesis, he will only obtain for the orange a remunerative price. I leave to the Fair Traders the task of drawing the conclusion.

4th. If I have insisted upon this distinction between the conditions of production and the conditions of sale—a distinction which the Fair Traders will, without doubt, find paradoxical—I have done so to lead up to another statement, that after equalising *the conditions of production, exchange* would not be *really free*. I must be permitted to follow my argument to the end : I will not be long.

Will you consent to assume for a moment that the average rate of wages of daily labour in England is three shillings per man. It will incontestably follow that to produce *directly* an orange in England, will cost one-third of a day's labour, or its equivalent, while to produce the value of a Portuguese orange will cost only one thirty-sixth of a day's labour, which is saying, in other words, that the sun does in Lisbon what labour does in Cornwall. But is it not evident that if I can produce an orange, or, what comes to the same thing, if I can buy an orange, with a thirty-sixth of a day's work, I am placed relatively to this production exactly under the same conditions as the Portuguese producer himself, deducting the cost of transit, which ought, of course, to be at my charge? It then is certain that Free Trade equalises the conditions of production, directly or indirectly, as much as they are capable of being equalised, since it leaves no other existing inequality but the inevitable difference of the cost of transport.

I add that Free Trade equalises all the conditions of enjoyments, of comforts, and of consumption; this, which we never take into consideration, is, however, the essential part, since definitely consumption is the final aim of all our industrial efforts. With freedom of exchange, we are able to enjoy the fruits of the Portuguese sun equally with the Portuguese himself.

5th. This might suffice, but I will go further. I assert, and with full conviction, that if two countries find themselves placed in conditions of unequal production, *that of the two, the one which is the least favoured by nature has the most to gain from freedom of exchange.*

Really the whole question rests upon this point, and in elucidating it I shall have an opportunity of expounding an economic law of the highest importance, which, if well comprehended, seems to be destined to bring over all those who in our day are seeking, by what they designate as Fair Trade, to promote commercial prosperity. I mean the law of consumption, which the greater part of the Fair Traders may, perhaps, be reproached for having too much neglected.

Consumption is *the end*, the final object to which all economic phenomena converge, and it is, consequently, in consumption that their definitive solution is to be found.

All circumstances which favour production are welcomed by the producer, for *the immediate effect* is to enable him to demand a greater remuneration for himself; all circumstances which are adverse to production distress the producer, for *the immediate effect* is to limit his employment, and consequently his remuneration.

When a workman is able to improve the manipulation of

his particular branch of industry, the *immediate* advantage is reaped by himself. This is necessary, in order to induce him to turn his attention to the subject; and it is just, because his effort should have its recompense.

How does a new discovery operate? A man discovers a new mechanical process. *At first* he is enriched and others impoverished.

But the discovery becomes known; others imitate him. Their profits are at first considerable. They gain much, but they gain less than the inventor, for *competition* is awakened and begins its work. The price is lowered. The profits of the imitators diminish in proportion as the period from the time of the invention lengthens — that is to say, in proportion as imitation becomes less meritorious. The new industry soon arrives at its normal state; in other words, the remuneration is regulated by *the general rate of profits.* But how does this show itself? By the cheapness of the article produced. And for whose benefit? For the benefit of the consumer, *i.e.*, of society generally. The producers who thenceforward have no particular and exclusive merit, receive no longer an exclusive remuneration. As consumers, they without doubt participate in the advantages which the invention has conferred on the community. But this is all. Inasmuch as they are producers, they have fallen again under the ordinary conditions common to all the producers in the country. Society pays them for their work, but no longer for the utility of the invention. That has become the common and free heritage of the whole of the human race.

This is true of all the instruments of labour, from the nail and the hammer, to the locomotive engine and the electric telegraph. Society enjoys all through the abundance of consumption, and *enjoys it gratuitously*, because their effect is to diminish the price of articles, and all that part of the price which has been annihilated, which represents the work of the inventor in the production, evidently renders the production in that degree *gratuitous*. The only thing remaining to be paid for is the manual labour. I send for a workman, he comes with his saw, I pay him three shillings per day, and he saws for me twenty-five planks. If the saw had not been invented he would not perhaps have fashioned one, and I should not the less have paid him for his day's work. The *usefulness* of the saw is then a gratuitous gift to me; it is a portion of the heritage which I have received *in common* with other men from the intelligence of our ancestors. I have two labourers in my field; the one holds the handle of the plough, the other the handle of the spade. The result of their work is very different, but the price of the day's labour of each is the same, because remuneration is not in proportion to the utility of the product of labour, but to the effort—to the labour required.

I entreat the patience of the reader a little further, and beg him to believe that I have not lost sight of my subject—commercial freedom. But he must allow me to recapitulate the conclusion at which I have arrived. *Remuneration is not measured by the utility of the works which the producer brings to market, but by the cost of his labour.**

I have taken my examples mainly from human inventions. Let us now refer more especially to natural advantages. In all production nature and man co-operate. But the useful part which nature performs is always gratuitous ; only that part which is due to human labour forms the object of exchange, and consequently of remuneration. This remuneration no doubt varies very much, by reason of the intensity of the labour, the skill, the promptitude, and the aptitude of the workmen, of the need for it at the time, of the temporary absence of rivalry, and other circumstances. But it is not the less true in principle that the part produced by the co-operation of natural forces, since it belongs to all, does not in any degree enter into the price of the product.

We do not pay for the light of the sun, because nature gives it. We pay for that of electricity, of gas, of tallow, of oil, of wax, because in these cases there is human labour to be remunerated ; and we must remark, that it is entirely the work and not its utility to which remuneration is proportioned, so that it may very well happen that one of these illuminating powers, though much more intense than another, may, however, cost less. It would be sufficient for this result that the same quantity of human labour could furnish more of this product than of the other.

When a Water Company supplies my house with water, if

---

* It is true that labour does not receive a uniform remuneration. There are different kinds of labour, more or less intense, dangerous, skilful, &c. Competition establishes in each case a current price, and it is of this variable price that I speak.

I were to pay for it with regard to the *absolute utility* of the water, my fortune would not suffice. But I pay on account of the trouble which the company has taken in bringing it. The water is not really the subject of our bargain, but the labour required for obtaining the water. Tropical countries are very favourable to the production of sugar and coffee. This is the same as saying that nature does the greater part of the work, and leaves little to be done by manual labour. But then, who reaps the advantages of this liberality of nature? Not those countries—for competition obliges them to receive only remuneration for the manual labour—but mankind in general; for the result of this liberality is *cheapness*, and cheapness belongs to all the world. Thus the bounties of nature, as well as improvements made in the processes of production, are, or are constantly tending to become, under the law of competition, the common and *gratuitous* patrimony of consumers, of the mass of mankind.

The countries which do not possess these advantages have, therefore, everything to gain by exchanging with those which do possess them, because exchange is made between *the amounts of labour and labour*, the portion of usefulness derived from nature which these works include being deducted. And they are evidently the most favoured countries which have incorporated in a given amount of human labour the most of these *natural advantages*. Their products, representing less labour, are less highly paid for; in other terms, they are cheaper, and if all the liberality of nature resolves itself into *cheapness*, evidently it is not the country producing, but the country consuming, which reaps the benefit of it.

A is a favoured country, B is a country less favoured by nature. Exchange is the barter of *value*, and the value being reduced by competition to represent labour, exchange is the barter of equal amounts of labour. What nature has done for the productions exchanged is given in one shape or another *gratuitously*, and over and above the purchase value. Hence it follows strictly, that to exchange with countries most favoured by nature is most advantageous; and that whereas countries which levy duties upon foreign produce benefit by this gratuitous assistance of nature less the amount of the duties they levy, countries which have free ports benefit by the full value of it.

CHAPTER VI.

OUR PRODUCTIONS ARE BURDENED WITH RATES AND TAXES.

THAT our productions are burdened with rates and taxes, is a part of the same fallacy. You demand that foreign productions should be taxed, in order to neutralise the effects of the rates and taxes which press heavily on our home productions. The question still is, how to equalise the conditions of production. We need only say one word on this head, which is, that the rate or tax is an artificial obstacle, which has exactly the same result as a natural obstacle—that of forcing a rise in price. If this rise arrives at such a point that there is more loss in creating the production than in obtaining it from abroad, by applying our industry to the production of other things to exchange for it, private interest will soon learn to choose the lesser of two evils. I might, therefore, send the reader back to the preceding demonstration; but the fallacy which I have here to combat recurs so often in the dolorous lamentations of the "Fair Trade" school, that it well deserves a special discussion.

If you speak of those few taxes which are laid on certain productions, I am ready to admit that it is reasonable to subject foreign produce to them. For example : it would be absurd to take off the duty from tobacco or foreign spirits. Tobacco is not produced in this country, and the tax protects no one. On spirits manufactured in England we levy a tax (Excise) equivalent to the duty on foreign spirits. Here again the tax protects no one. These are circumstances under which I admit of a duty, *not protective* but fiscal, being placed on foreign productions.*

But to assert that a country should, because she is subjected

---

* The Fair Trade manifesto quotes with approval the following words from Mr. Mill :—"A country cannot be expected to renounce the power of taxing foreigners, unless foreigners will in return practice towards itself the same forbearance. The only mode in which a country can save itself from being a loser by the revenue duties imposed by other countries on its commodities, is to impose corresponding revenue duties on theirs." I would point out that by revenue duties Mr. Mill means duties levied not for protective, but for fiscal purposes—duties which, if levied upon foreign goods, would also be levied upon the same articles produced at home.

C

to heavier rates and taxes than neighbouring nations, protect herself by her tariff from the competition of her rivals, is a fallacy, which I intend to assail.

The State may make a good or a bad use of its taxes. It makes a good use when it renders services to the public equivalent in value to what the public gives ; it makes a bad use of them when it expends this value without giving anything in return.

In the first case, to say that taxes place the country that pays them in a more unfavourable condition for production than that which is free from them, is a fallacy. We pay £6,500,000, it is true, for justice and police ; but we have justice and police, the security which they afford us, the time they save us ; and it is very probable that production is neither easier nor more active among people, if there be any such, where each takes the law into his own hands. I grant that we pay several millions in local rates for roads, bridges, and schools; but then we possess these roads, these bridges, and these schools, and unless it should be asserted that their cost is a wasteful expenditure, nobody can say that they render us inferior to those people who have none. Taxes well employed, far from injuring, help the *means of production.*

Those taxes (if there be any) which are unproductive, abolish if you can ; but it is the strangest way that can be imagined of neutralising their effects to add other taxes. If we are taxed needlessly already, surely that is the strongest reason why we should not tax ourselves still more?

There is no doubt that a retaliatory duty is a tax which, directed against a foreign product, really falls upon the home consumer (p. 28) ; and as the consumer is the tax-payer, is it endurable to address him in these terms : " Because the rates and taxes are heavy, we are going to put on more"?

Protection might, without changing its nature or results, take the form of a direct tax, levied by the State upon all, and distributed by it in indemnifying premiums to the privileged branches of industry.

Let us assume that foreign tin can be sold in our market at £50 a ton and no lower, and English tin at £60 a ton as the lowest price.

Under this hypothesis there will be two ways for the State to insure the home market to the home producer.

The first would be to place a duty of £12 a ton upon foreign tin. It is clear that it would thus be excluded, since it could not be sold for less than £62—viz., £50 for the remunerative price, and £12 for the tax ; and at this price it would be shut out from the market by English tin, which we have assumed to be at £60. In this case, the buyer, the consumer, will have paid all the cost of Protection.

The State might also levy a tax upon the public, and distribute it in premiums to the tin smelters at the rate of £12 a ton. The protective result would be the same. Foreign tin would be equally excluded ; for our tin smelters would sell at £48, which, with the £12 premium, would give them a remunerative price of £60 ; and with tin in the market at £48, the foreigner could not sell his at £50.

I can only see one point of difference between these two systems. The principle is the same, the result is the same ; only in the one case the protective duty is paid by the consumers of the article, in the other by all the tax-payers.

I confess frankly my predilection for the second system. It appears to me more just, more economical, and more straightforward—more just, because, if society wishes to give a largess to some of its members, all should contribute towards it ; more economical, because it would save much expense in collecting, and would do away with many impediments ; in fine, more straightforward, because the public would see the operation clearly, and know what it was being made to do.

But if the protective system had taken this form, would it not be rather laughable to hear people say, " We pay heavy taxes for the army, the navy, justice, public works, the debt, &c.—it exceeds £83,000,000 ; for this very reason it is desirable that the State should take another dozen millions from us, to assist those poor iron companies which are unable to pay any dividends, those unfortunate ribbon makers at Coventry, those useful cotton spinners at Preston "?

If it be narrowly looked at, you may be assured that this is what the fallacy I am combating leads to. Your efforts will be in vain ; you cannot *give money* to some without taking it from others. If you mean absolutely to impoverish the contributor, well and good ; but, it is like mockery to say to him, " I am taking still more from you, to compensate for what I have already taken."

You take advantage of England's being heavily burdened

C 2

with rates and taxes to deduce from it that you must protect such or such branches of industry. But we have to pay these taxes in spite of your duties. If, then, the representative of a branch of industry were to come before you, and say, "I am made to join in the payment of taxes ; that raises the cost price of my productions, and I ask for a retaliatory duty to raise also the selling price ;" what else does he ask but that his part of the taxes should fall upon the rest of the community ? His purpose is to recover, by the enhanced price of his productions, the amount of his share of taxation. Now, the whole of the taxes being paid into the Treasury, and the mass of the people being subject to this rise in price, they pay both their own share of the tax and also that of this branch of industry. But you say, "We will protect everybody." In the first place, such a thing is impossible ; and even were it possible, of what advantage would it be ? "I will pay for you, you shall pay for me, but anyhow the tax must be paid."

Thus you are the dupes of an illusion. You pay taxes and rates in order to have an army, a navy, judges, roads, &c., and afterwards you wish to free from its share of taxation first one branch of industry, then a second, then a third, always distributing the burden among the mass of the people ; but you do nothing except create interminable complications, without any other result than the existence of these complications. Prove to me that the rise of price, owing to retaliatory duties, would fall upon the foreigner, and I might see something valid in your argument. But if it is true that the English public paid taxes before the retaliatory duties were imposed, and that subsequent to the imposition of the duties it pays at once the retaliatory duties and the taxes, in truth I do not see what is gained by it.

But I go much further. I say that the more heavily taxed we are, the more eager we ought to be to open our ports to the foreigner who may be less burdened than ourselves. And why ? To lay upon him a greater part of our burden. It cannot be too often repeated that it is an incontestable axiom in political economy that taxes upon imports fall upon the consumer.

[But, I may ask, is it altogether true that England, as compared with other countries, is heavily burdened with rates and taxes ? A table compiled by Mr. Mulhall (Balance-Sheet of the World) shows that far from this being the case, there is no other country in Europe (with the exceptions of Denmark, Norway, and Sweden) less heavily taxed than England. And even the United States, a country often spoken of as if it were free from the burden of rates and taxes, has, in this respect, an advantage over us of only about 2½ per cent.

NATIONAL AND LOCAL TAXATION COMPARED WITH EARNINGS IN 1880.

Great Britain ...	...	...	...	...	11·88
Europe ...	..	...	...	...	15·38
United States ...	..	...	...	...	9·21
South Africa ...	...	...	...	...	19·60
South America .	...	...	...	...	19·25]

CHAPTER VII.

IMPORTS AND EXPORTS.

"IT is a fact of grave importance," say the Fair Traders, "that the amount of imports is continually increasing, and vastly exceeds the amount of exports; every year England buys more foreign productions, and sells in proportion fewer home productions. Do not the figures prove it? What do we see? In 1880 the imports exceeded the exports by nearly £200,000,000.* These facts indicate to us that national labour *is not sufficiently protected*, that the competition of our rivals *oppresses* our national industry. Economists have declared that when we buy we necessarily sell a corresponding portion of our merchandise—in fact, that the more we buy the more we sell. But this cannot be true. It is evident that we are buying, not with our ordinary productions, not with our revenue, not with the fruits of our permanent labour, but with our capital, with our accumulated savings, which should serve for reproduction. Every year

* This is the estimate adopted by Sir E. Sullivan and by many other Fair Traders. The sum of £200,000,000 is arrived at by excluding from the exports of Great Britain our outward shipments of foreign and Colonial produce, which is absurd. The returns for 1880 are as follows:—

Total Imports ...	...	...	...	...	...	£411,299,565
Exports of British produce		...	£223,060,446			
Ditto Foreign and Colonial		...	£63,354,020			
Total Exports ...	...	...	...	...	...	£286,414,466
Excess of Imports over Exports			...			£124,815,099

we are giving nearly £200,000,000 to foreigners.   If this
continue, we march headlong to ruin, and entirely destroy the
national capital."

Well, these are men with whom it is possible to come to
an understanding.   There is no hypocrisy in this language.
The theory of the balance of trade is most plainly acknow-
ledged in it.   England imports £200,000,000 more than she
exports ;   therefore England loses £200,000,000 a year.   And
the remedy?—is to prevent importation.   This conclusion
cannot be avoided.

Political Economists will doubtless blame me for arguing
against the balance of imports by exports.   To combat the
theory of the balance of trade, they would say, is fighting
with a shadow.

However, not to fatigue my readers, I need not examine
this theory too closely.   I will content myself with submitting
it to the test of facts.

Our principles are constantly accused of being only good
in theory.   But tell me, gentlemen, do you believe that
merchants' account-books are good in practice?   It appears to
me that if there is anything in the world which has a practical
authority, when it is a question of profit and loss, it is traders'
account-books.   It is very unlikely that all the merchants in the
world should for ages have come to an agreement together to
keep their books in such a manner that they show to them
their profits as losses and their losses as profits.

Now, one of my mercantile friends, having entered into
two transactions,. the results of which have been very different,
I have been curious to compare on this head the accounts of
the counting-house with those of the Custom House.

Mr. Smith dispatched a ship from Liverpool to the United
States laden with English hardware to the amount of £10,000.
This was the declared value at the Custom House.   On its
arrival at New Orleans it was found that the cargo had in-
curred 10 per cent. of charges, and it paid 25 per cent. in
duty, which made it amount to £13,500.   It was sold at 20
per cent. profit, say £2,000, and produced a total of £15,500.
After paying the charges, £1,000, and the duty, £2,500, Mr.
Smith had £12,000 to receive.   This he invested in cotton.
The cotton also incurred for transport, insurance, commission,
&c., 10 per cent. of charges, so that at the moment it entered
Liverpool the new cargo amounted to £13,200, and this was

the value set down in the Custom House lists.   To conclude, Mr. Smith realised again upon this return cargo 20 per cent. profit, say £2,400 ; in other words, the cotton was sold for £15,600.

The books of Mr. Smith show him on the *credit side* of the account of *profits and losses*, as gains, two items, one of £2,000, the other of £2,400, and Mr. Smith is convinced that in this respect his accounts do not deceive him.

But what do the figures that the Custom House has set down in reference to this transaction say ?   They say that England has exported £10,000 and imported £13,200 ; from which it is concluded " *that she has wasted her past savings, that she has impoverished herself, that she is marching headlong to ruin, that she has given £3,200 of her capital to the foreigner.*"*

Some time after, Mr. Smith dispatched another vessel, likewise laden with £10,000 worth of our national productions. But the unhappy ship foundered on quitting the port, and nothing remained for Mr. Smith to do but to enter into his books two little items thus worded :—

" *Sundry merchandise, debtor to X, £*10,000 for the purchase of various articles shipped in the vessel N.

" *Profit and loss, debtor to sundry merchandise, £*10,000 *for the total and complete loss* of the cargo."

In the meantime, the Custom House for its part inscribed £10,000 in its table of *exports*, and as it will never have anything in return to set down in the table of *imports*, it follows that this shipwreck brings *a clear net profit* of £10,000 to England.

There is also this conclusion to be drawn from it—that, according to the theory of the balance of trade, England possesses a very simple means of doubling her capital at any

---

* Mr. Cross, in a speech delivered in the House of Commons (12th Aug., 1881), gave three illustrations drawn from foreign trade, showing the profits made on the exportation of cargoes of cotton, iron, and coal respectively.   In each case Mr. Cross spoke as if the charges payable upon the outward shipments went to swell the amount of the homeward investment.   This is evidently incorrect.   It would be the same as saying that " Mr. Smith " invested in his return shipment the full amount that he received for his cargo, viz., £15,500, instead of allowing for his paying away £3,500 of it in charges and duty.   The homeward cargo is equal to the cost of the outward cargo plus the profit only. The illustrations given by Mr. Cross were also imperfect by reason of his omitting to allow any sum as *profit* on the transactions.   Upon this oversight of Mr. Cross's some Fair Traders have fastened, and have endeavoured to prove from it that our imports should only exceed our exports by the merest fraction, which is absurd.

minute. It would only be necessary for her to pass it all through the Custom House and throw it into the sea.

In this case the exports will be equal in amount to her capital; the imports will be *nil*, and we shall gain all that the ocean has swallowed up.

Of course this is too palpably ridiculous to be advanced by the "Fair Traders;" it is, however, what their argument comes to, and they seek to give effect to it.

The truth is, that we must take the balance of trade *the contrary way*, and calculate our national profit from foreign commerce by the excess of imports over exports. This excess, the charges being deducted, forms the actual gain. And this theory, which is the true one, leads directly to Free Trade.

Exaggerate this theory as much as you will; it has nothing to dread from being submitted to the process. Suppose even, if it would amuse you, that the foreigner inundated us with all kinds of useful merchandise, without asking anything in return; that our imports were *infinite* and our exports *nil;* I still defy you to prove that we shall be poorer in consequence.

[Driven from this position, the Fair Traders say that, inundated by foreign produce, we are being stripped of all our money to pay for it. "We are buying food from abroad faster than we are making money to pay for it," says Sir E. Sullivan. But this is not so. During the last ten years (1871-81) we have imported more gold and silver than we have exported by £36,000,000. Clearly we have not paid for our imports with precious metals. "Then," say the Fair Traders, "you are paying for them by sending abroad foreign bonds." This is equally untrue; for whereas twenty years ago we were computed to possess £1,000,000,000 of the world's obligations in our strong-box, bankers who collect the dividends tell us that at the present time the indebtedness of foreign countries to England has enormously increased. "But," say the Fair Traders, "how do you account for *this* fact? In 1873—a year of great prosperity—the imports, instead of exceeding the exports by nearly £200,000,000, exceeded them by little more than £100,000,000." The answer is simple: at that time we were lending to foreign countries at the rate of more than £100,000,000 a year.

"How does capital *get* abroad," the *Spectator* enquired, a short time ago, "without something like an excess of exports over imports?" The following illustration from the

Board of Trade returns will explain. In 1880, 587,000 tons of coal, valued at £265,000, were exported to India, where, after paying all charges, they realised £900,000. This sum purchased 60,000 tons of jute, the value of which on arrival here was £1,080,000. The coal left this country valued at £265,000; its equivalent, the jute, came home valued at £1,080,000. Now, suppose that we had wanted to lend India that year half a million. Instead of investing the £900,000 in jute, £500,000 of that amount would have been handed over as a loan, and £400,000 would have remained over for investment in jute. This, on arrival in England would have been valued at £480,000. We should still show exports £265,000, imports £480,000, an excess of imports over exports of £215,000, although in this very transaction we had lent India half a million sterling.

When investigating tables of imports and exports, we must be on our guard against supposing that they necessarily render a complete account of the *course* of trade. Let me illustrate this. In the published returns we appear to have exported to France (1880) produce to the value of £28,000,000, and to have imported from that country produce to the value of £42,000,000. The same returns show that in that year we exported to Belgium produce to the value of £13,000,000, and imported goods to the value of £11,250,000. The explanation is, that whereas almost the whole of the produce we take from France comes to us direct from that country, a considerable portion of the produce we send her in exchange, coming from the north of England, goes through Belgium, and so appears in the tables as if it were exported to Belgium, whereas it is really exported not to Belgium but to France.

But it may not unfrequently happen that a country *does* export more to another country than it imports from it, not merely in appearance—as in the case of our trade with Belgium—but as a fact. The United States export considerably more to England (chiefly food) than they import from us. China exports largely of tea and silk to the United States, but takes scarcely any American produce. India again exports largely to China (mainly opium) and takes very little in return. The result is, that England becomes indebted to the United States, the United States to China, and China to India, and accounts between the four countries are settled by England sending to India large amounts of cotton goods.]

CHAPTER VIII.

PETITION OF THE TALLOW-CHANDLERS, LAMPMAKERS, AND OTHERS.

" To the honourable the members of the House of Commons :

" We are suffering from the intolerable competition of a foreign rival, who is placed, as it seems to us, in a condition so infinitely superior to ours for the production of light, that he *inundates* our *national market* at a marvellously reduced price; for as soon as he shows himself our sale ceases, all consumers apply to him, and a branch of English industry of which the ramifications are innumerable is immediately thrown into a state of complete stagnation. We pray that you will be pleased to make a law ordering that all windows, skylights, inside and outside shutters, curtains, fan-lights, bulls'-eyes, carriage-blinds, in short, that all openings, holes, chinks, and crevices should be closed, by which the light of the sun can penetrate into houses to the injury of the flourishing trades with which we have endowed our country, which cannot now, without ingratitude, abandon us to so unequal a contest.

" In the first place, if you shut out as much as possible all access to natural light, if you thus create the necessity for artificial light, what English industry exists which will not in some measure be encouraged ?

" If more electric light is needed, more machinery must be constructed. If more gas is required, more coal must be raised.

" If more tallow is consumed, more oxen and sheep must be bred and reared, and, in consequence, more meadows will be cultivated; there will be more meat, more wool, more hides, and, above all, more manure, which is the foundation of all agricultural riches.

" The same results will follow to our navigation : thousands of vessels will be engaged in whale-fishing, and in a short time we shall have a greatly strengthened marine, capable of upholding the honour of England against all comers.

" And further, in articles of London and Birmingham manufacture, consider how many gilt, bronze and glass chandeliers, lamps, lustres, and candelabra must burn in the spacious warehouses which will then take the place of our present shops.

"Consider the matter, gentlemen, and you must be convinced that there will be scarcely an Englishman, from the most wealthy coal-master to the most humble matchseller, whose condition will not be ameliorated through the success of our petition.

"Gentlemen, we foresee your objections, but you will be unable to bring forward one which is not to be found in the works of the partisans of Free Trade.

"If you tell us that, although *we* may gain by this Protection, England will be no gainer, because the consumer will be burdened with the cost, we shall reply that 'you have no right to consider the interests of the consumer. You should sacrifice them in all cases where they are opposed to those of the producer, in order to *encourage industry*—to extend the boundaries of industry.'

"Do you say that the light of the sun is a gratuitous gift, and that to reject gratuitous gifts is to reject wealth itself, under the pretext of encouraging the means of acquiring it? But this is the very reason why we desire Protection to native industry, and the *more so in proportion as foreign produce approximates* to gratuitous gifts.

"Labour and nature are united in different proportions, according to country and climate, in order to create a production.

"The part which nature contributes is always gratuitous; it is the part which is added by labour which gives to the production its value, and requires payment.

"If a Lisbon orange is sold at one-twelfth of a Cornish orange, it is because a natural and therefore gratuitous heat ripens the one, while the other is forced by an artificial and therefore expensive heat.

"Consequently, when an orange arrives from Portugal, we can say that eleven-twelfths of it is given to us gratuitously, and one-twelfth as a return for labour; or, in other terms, it is given to us for one-twelfth the price relatively to those of Cornwall.

"Again, when a product—tin, sugar, wheat, or cloth—comes to us from abroad, and we can obtain it with less labour than if we made it ourselves, the difference is a gratuitous gift which is conferred on us. This gift is more or less considerable, in proportion as the difference is more or less great. It will be the quarter, the half, or three-quarters of the value of the production, according as the foreigner asks us three-quarters, a half, or a quarter as much as it would cost if home manufactured. It is as complete as it can be when the giver, as in the case of the sun giving light, asks no payment. The question—and we put it formally—is, whether you wish to give to England the benefit of a gratuitous consumption, or the supposed advantages of a laborious production? Choose, but be consistent; for if you would reject tin, sugar, wheat, woollens, and other foreign stuffs, *in proportion* as their price approximates to *zero*, is it not absurd to admit the light of the sun, of which the price is at *zero*, during the whole day?"

We may smile, and remember that winter fogs in London sometimes accomplish for vendors of artificial light what this petition demands. The loss the grocer suffered when his pane of glass was broken (p. 11) is precisely similar to that which the community suffers from the loss of the sun's light on these occasions.

I am also reminded that when shoe-ties came into fashion in the last century, and replaced buckles, the bucklemakers of Birmingham petitioned Parliament to make the wearing of buckles compulsory.

CHAPTER IX.

DIFFERENTIAL DUTIES AND A BUND WITH THE COLONIES.

*A poor husbandman dwelling near Bordeaux raised a vine with great care. After much anxiety and labour, he produced a cask of wine, and in the satisfaction which he felt he no longer remembered that he had earned it by the sweat of his brow.

" I will sell it," he said to his wife, " and with the proceeds I will buy yarn, with which you can make your daughter's *trousseau.*" The good countryman went to the town, where he met a Belgian and an Englishman. The Belgian said to him, " Give me your cask of wine, and in exchange I will give you fifteen packets of yarn." The Englishman said, " Give me your wine, and I will give you twenty packets of yarn, for we English

---

* As we levy no duties upon foreign or colonial produce, whether differential or for the purposes of Protection, or, what is the same thing, of Reciprocity, the above illustration has been left unchanged.

spin cheaper than the Belgians." But a Custom House officer who was present objected. "My fine fellow," said he, "exchange with the Belgian if you please, but it is my business to prevent your exchanging with the Englishman." "What!" said the countryman, "you expect me to be satisfied with fifteen packets of thread from Brussels when I can have twenty from Manchester?" "Certainly; do you not see that France would lose if you receive twenty packets instead of fifteen?" "It is hard for me to understand," said the wine-grower ——, "And for me to explain," replied the Custom House officer; "but it is certain—for all the deputies, ministers, and journalists are agreed on this point—that the more a people receives in exchange for a certain quantity of its produce the more it is impoverished." He was forced to exchange with the Belgian. The husbandman's daughter had only three-quarters of her *trousseau*, and the good people cannot yet understand how ruin could ensue from receiving four instead of three, and how they can be richer with three dozen napkins than with four dozen.

[Now, suppose that the Custom House officer had been instructed to levy such a duty upon fifteen packets of English yarn as would make their cost, with the duty, the same as fifteen packets of Belgian yarn; and, further, suppose that the husbandman still preferred to purchase the English yarn; then, I ask, what useful service would the Custom House officer have performed?] Absolutely none. The husbandman might as well have given the amount of the duty to a thief. It is inconsequent to say that the Government will spend this money to the great profit of *national labour;* the thief would have done the same, and so would the husbandman if he had not been stopped on the road by the lawful highwayman.

[The manifesto of the Fair Traders tells us that "foreign nations do not tax their consumers by taxing British commodities." There is but one inference to be drawn from this—that if we taxed foreign commodities we should not thereby be taxing our consumers. I wonder what the husbandman would say to this?

But while the Fair Trade manifesto only leaves us to infer this, Lord Randolph Churchill states it explicitly. He says:— "Tax the skilled labour of the foreigner, tax imports, and bestow the large profits in aid of the relief of local taxation." He clearly differs entirely in opinion from the Bordeaux hus-

bandman, and evidently believes that taxes upon imports fall
not upon the consumer but upon the producer. We import
£400,000,000 annually: why not, then, tax the foreigner 50
per cent.? We should raise £200,000,000 a year! If any
one still entertains a doubt as to who pays the tax—the consumer or the producer—the following illustration, given by
Mr. J. K. Cross, may help him to solve it :—

"We send salt to Russia. At Nantwich it is worth 10s.
a ton, and at the port of Hull, free on board, say 15s. a ton.
It goes to St. Petersburg or to Odessa, and on arrival is taxed
£2 10s. a ton. Who pays that? The salt is worth 10s. a ton
in Cheshire. Can it be that the salt pays the 50s. tax, or the
man who makes it? The salt only costs 10s.: how can it be
said that this tax is paid by us?"

In addition to their proposals for retaliatory duties, the
Fair Traders further suggest that we should do well to establish
differential duties in favour of our colonies. They propose
that "all tariffs should be abolished throughout the empire,
and that an Imperial Fiscal or Customs Union should be established." This is a matter of great importance to England,
as it is sought to establish differential duties, which differ from
protective duties only in this—that they would be adopted not
for the supposed advantage of the home population, but in the
interests of our colonists.

In order to understand the loss which differential duties in
favour of the colonies would cause to the home population, we
have only to suppose ourselves in the position of the French
husbandman in the foregoing dialogue, and substitute for
the Belgian a West Indian sugar planter, for the Englishman a French sugar merchant, and for the yarn, the subject of the bargain, a certain number of barrels of sugar.
We shall then be in a position to understand the injury
which the Fair Traders are asking us to do to ourselves, in
favour of a part of our fellow-subjects, who cannot be said
to take any part in sustaining the national burdens. In 1845
we did indeed maintain in favour of our colonies a differential
duty against foreign sugar. It was sufficient to enable the
British plantation sugar, though 16s. per cwt. higher in price
than foreign sugar of the same quality, to monopolise the
home market. And in that year alone English sugar consumers paid for their sugar, by reason of the differential
duty, £3,000,000 more than they would otherwise have

done, no part of which reached the public Treasury, and every penny of which was a dead loss to the community.

To this system we are now invited to return. Differential duties are to be re-established, and the home consumers are to suffer loss for the benefit of our colonial producers.

But this is not all. By the re-imposition of differential duties there would be not only a loss to *consumers* but to *producers* also, who would suffer in a multitude of ways. " England," says Mr. J. K. Cross,* " is now the emporium of the world ; she has no rival. Men who want the best market come here to buy. But the Fair Traders would stop this. The foreign merchant now comes here from Brazil, from Peru, or the colonial merchant from Canada or the Cape, and buys all he wants in London, whether it be the artificial flowers of France, the gloves of France or Austria, Sweden or Germany, Yeovil or Leicester—he finds them all in Wood Street ; the silks of France, Switzerland, and Italy, in Fore Street, or in St. Paul's Churchyard, and with the English silks as well ; and having made his purchases of these wares, he buys his cottons, his linens, his woollens, his small wares, and his hosiery, of the English manufacturers, and as shipping is direct from London and Liverpool to all the world, he ships his parcel, which, being well bought, he knows will be well sold. By differential duties we shall keep these and other things out of the market ; but they will still be made : and those who now come here to buy will go elsewhere, and they will then buy more of foreign things than they do now. We shall force the foreigner to buy past us, and by forcing him to buy his cloths and silks from others, it is a thousand to one he will buy from them some other things which he has hitherto bought from the English. We should, moreover, lose the profit on carriage and sale of foreign goods in our efforts to tax the labour of the foreigner."]

* Speech at Oldham, Dec. 8, 1831. Circulated by the *Cobden Club*.

CHAPTER X.

RECIPROCITY.

WE have seen that all which serves to make transport difficult acts in the same manner as Protection ; or, to put the converse, that Protection acts in the same manner as conditions which render transport difficult.

Thus we may truly call a tariff, a marsh, a rut, a ravine, a steep declivity—in short, an *obstacle*, which has the effect of augmenting the difference between the price of consumption and the cost of production. In like manner, it is evident that a marsh and a bog are in fact equivalent to protective duties.

An obstacle, although it may be artificial, is still an obstacle, and for the same reason that a canal is more advantageous than a sandy, mountainous, and ill-made road, so our welfare is more consulted by Free Trade than by Protection.

But " Fair Traders" say, this liberty must be reciprocal. If we remove our restrictions from France, when France does not remove hers from us, we are losers. We must make a *treaty of commerce* upon the basis of reciprocity ; we must make mutual concessions ; we must make a *sacrifice* in buying, in order to have the advantage in selling.

Those who reason thus—I am sorry to be obliged to tell them so—hold, knowingly or unknowingly, the principles of Protection, only they are a little more inconsistent than absolute Protectionists.

I will demonstrate this by means of a fable.

DULLTOWN AND BRISKTOWN.

There were—it does not signify how situated—two towns, Dulltown and Brisktown. At a great expense they constructed a road joining the two towns. When it was made, Dulltown said, " Brisktown is inundating me with her produce ; I must consider about it." In consequence, she created and paid a body of *preventives*—so called because their business was to put obstacles in the way of the arrival of goods from Brisktown. Soon afterwards, Brisktown had her body of *preventives* as well.

After the lapse of several centuries, intelligence having made great progress, Brisktown became sufficiently enlightened to see that these reciprocal obstacles were only reciprocal annoyances. She sent a diplomatist to Dulltown, whose speech, stript of its official phraseology, was as follows:—

"We constructed a road, and now we put hindrances on this same road. This is absurd ; we had better have left things as they were ; we should not then have had to pay for making a road, and then for the impediments which we have placed there. I have come to propose to you, in the name of Brisktown, not that we should at once remove the obstacles which we have mutually opposed to each other—to do so would be acting on principle, and we despise principle as much as you do—but to lessen some few of these obstacles, taking care to balance equally our respective *sacrifices* in so doing."

Thus spoke the diplomatist. Dulltown asked time for reflection. She consulted her manufacturers and agriculturists by turns. At last, at the end of several years, she declared that the negotiations were broken off.

After this news, the inhabitants of Brisktown held a council. An old man (who had been always suspected of having been secretly bought by Dulltown) rose and said,—

"The obstacles created by Dulltown injure our sales ; it is a misfortune : those which we have created ourselves injure our purchases ; this is another misfortune. We can do nothing in the first case, but the second depends upon ourselves. Let us relieve ourselves from the one, although we cannot be quit of both. Let us abolish our preventive service, without requiring Dulltown to do the same. At some future day she will doubtless know her own interests better."

Another councillor, a practical man, free from principles, who had thriven on the experience of his ancestors, exclaimed, "Do not let us listen to this dreamer, this theorist, this innovator, this economist. We should be ruined if the hindrances on the road between Dulltown and Brisktown were not equalised and balanced. There would be more difficulty in going than in coming; in exporting than in importing. Relatively to Dulltown, we should labour under the same disadvantages as Liverpool, Bristol, Hull, Glasgow, London, Newcastle, Hamburg, and New Orleans, when compared with the towns placed at the sources of the Mersey, the Severn, the Ouse, the Clyde, the Thames, the Tyne, the Elbe, and the

D

Mississippi ; for it is more difficult to ascend rivers than to descend them. (A voice : 'Towns at the mouths of rivers have flourished more than towns situated at their sources.') It is impossible. (The same voice : 'But it is so.') Well then, they have prospered *in opposition to all rules.*"

So conclusive a reason made the assembly waver. The orator settled their convictions by speaking of national independence, national honour, national dignity, and national industry, of the inundation of foreign produce, of taxes, and of ruinous competition—in short, he carried the vote for the continuance of the obstacles ; and, if you are curious, I can still take you to certain countries where you may see with your own eyes the road-maker and the officer of the *preventive* service working together on the best of terms, by order of the ·same legislative assembly, and at the expense of the same tax-payer—the one to clear the road, the other to put impediments upon it.

CHAPTER XI.

WILL RETALIATORY DUTIES RAISE THE RATE OF WAGES ?

WOULD you rightly appreciate the effect of retaliatory duties ? Then examine their influence upon the *abundance or scarcity of things*, and not upon *the rise or fall of prices.* Have no confidence in *prices*, for this would lead you into an inextricable labyrinth. You are asked to levy duties on foreign produce because it would enhance the price of home productions :—

"High prices increase the expense of living, and, *consequently*, the price of labour, and each regains in the increased price of his produce the increased amount of his expenses. Thus, if all pay as consumers, all receive as producers."

It is evident that we can reverse the argument, and say :—
"If all receive as producers, all pay as consumers."

Now, what does this prove ? Nothing, except that Protection displaces capital uselessly and unjustly, and so does spoliation.

. Again, in order to admit that this vast apparatus succeeds in providing compensation to the labourer, we must adhere to the "*consequently*," and believe that the price of labour rises with the price of protected produce. Such is not the case ; because I believe that the price of labour, as of everything else, is governed by the relation between supply and demand. I can well understand that restriction would diminish the supply of food and clothing, and consequently raise the price, but I do not so clearly see how it would increase the demand for labour, or, in other words, raise the rate of wages. Moreover I the less believe it because the demand for labour depends on the amount of disposable capital. Now, Protection may displace capital, may divert it from one industry to another, but cannot increase it to the amount of a single farthing.

This is a question of the highest interest, and I shall return to its consideration elsewhere. I go back to *prices*.

Suppose that an isolated nation, possessing a certain quantity of coin, chose to burn half its produce every year; I can prove, according to the theory stated above, that that country will not be less rich.

Indeed, in consequence of this burning, everything will be doubled in price, and the valuation made before and after the disaster will show the same nominal amount. But then, who will have lost ? If John buys his cloth dearer, he also sells his wheat dearer, and if Peter loses on his purchase of wheat he will retrieve his losses by the sale of his cloth. " Each regains in the enhanced price of his produce the increased amount of his expenditure, and if all pay as consumers, all receive as producers."

All this is mystification, and not science. The truth, reduced to its most simple expression, stands thus : whether men destroy a quantity of cloth or wheat by fire or by use, the effect is the same *as to price*, but not *as to capital*, for wealth or prosperity consists in having things for use.

In like manner, restriction, in diminishing the abundance of things, may raise the price, so that each person may be, if you please, as rich as regards money. Write, however, in an inventory, three quarters of wheat at 40s., or four at 30s.; the sum of both will be £6, but will the respective quantities equally supply the wants of the consumer ?

I shall not cease to bring back the Fair Trader to the subject as it affects consumers, for that is the end of all exertion, and the solution of all economic problems. I shall ask him again and again—Is it not true that restrictions, by preventing exchanges, by limiting the division of labour, and forcing it to be applied in overcoming the difficulties of situation and temperature, end in diminishing the quantity produced by any determinate amount of exertion? And of what advantage is it, if the less quantity, produced under the retaliatory system, has the same nominal value as the greater quantity, produced under the system of Free Trade? Man does not live on *nominal values*, but on real productions; and the more there are of these productions, no matter at what price, the richer he is.

If you would judge between the two doctrines, put them to the test of exaggeration.

According to the one doctrine, the English people would be quite as rich—that is to say, quite as well provided with every-thing—with the tenth part of their annual productions, because they would then become ten times more valuable.

According to our doctrine, the English people would be infinitely rich, if their annual productions were infinitely abundant, and consequently without any money value.

But is it true that retaliatory duties, which all confess raise the price of things, and thus injure the workman, compensate him at the same time by a proportionate rise in his wages?

On what depends the rate of wages?

When two workmen run after one master, wages fall; when two masters run after one workman, they rise.

Allow me, for the sake of brevity, to make use of the phrase which, although perhaps less clear, is more scientific :—
" The rate of wages depends on the relative proportions of the supply of and demand for labour."

But on what does the supply depend?

On the number of workmen in the market; and upon this element retaliatory duties can have no influence.

On what does the demand depend?

On the amount of disposable national capital. But under a system of retaliatory duties the law says, " You shall no longer receive such or such from the foreigner; it must be produced at home." Does that increase capital? Not in the least. It diverts it from one channel to another, but does not increase it by a farthing. It does not increase the demand for labour.

Such or such a manufactory is shown with pride. Has the capital by which it was established and is carried on fallen from the moon ?　No, it has been necessarily abstracted from that employed in agriculture, navigation, or other occupations.

I might descant much further on this subject, but I will now endeavour to make my meaning intelligible by an illustration.

A farmer had a farm of 200 acres, which he valued at £6,000.　As is the case with all farms, this farm was better adapted to produce certain articles of consumption than others. It was mainly a dairy farm—that is to say, it had rich pastures suitable for cattle—but a portion of it was also suitable for growing wheat and barley. It might, therefore, be called a mixed farm.　But a small portion of the corn, meat, butter, milk, and cheese which the farm produced sufficed to support the farmer and his family, and he sold the surplus in order to buy beer, clothes, &c.　The whole of his capital was distributed each year, in the form of wages, in the payment of tradesmen, and to the workmen in the neighbour-hood ; this capital was returned to him by the sale of produce, and, in fact, it increased from year to year, and the farmer, knowing well that unemployed capital gives no return, im-proved the condition of the working classes by means of his annual profits, which he used in improving his agricultural implements and in erecting improved buildings on his farm. He even placed some residue in the bank of the neighbouring town ; but here it did not remain idle in the strong-box, but was lent to ship-owners and to originators of useful works, so that it ended by being converted into wages.

In course of time the farmer died, and his son succeeded to his possessions.　"It must be confessed," said he, "that my father has been in error all his life.　He bought beer from the brewer ; he bought clothes from the draper and the tailor ; he paid tribute to the miller for grinding his corn, and to the tallow-chandler for his candles, while our servants could have brewed, could have ground our wheat, and could have made candles from the fat of the beasts.　Moreover, he could have grown flax, and our servants would have woven it ; he could have kept sheep, and our servants would have manufactured the wool into garments for our use.　He wasted his substance in giving to strangers wages which he could have easily distri-buted at home."

[Accordingly the son attempted to carry out in real life the charming, though uneconomic and anti-social, picture which Pope has drawn :—

" Happy the man whose wish and care
  A few paternal acres bound,
Content to breathe his native air
  In his own ground.
Whose herds with milk, whose fields with bread,
  Whose flocks supply him with attire,
Whose trees in summer yield him shade,
  In winter fire."]

Confident in his reasonings, he rearranged his farm. He divided it into many portions. In one he kept sheep. To feed them he grew turnips, and laid down part of his corn-land in pasture. He grew flax, he put up a mill, he purchased a loom, &c., &c. He thus provided for all the wants of his family, and made himself independent. He withdrew nothing from general circulation ; but neither did he add anything to it. Did he become richer ? No ; for the soil was not fitted for the cultivation of flax, it was not well suited for the breeding and rearing of sheep, and, in fact, the family was not so well supplied as when the father provided for them by means of exchange.

As for the workmen, there was no more work for them to do than there had been formerly ; there were certainly five times as many different things to be done, but then they were each employed but a fifth of their former time upon them. They made candles, but they grew less wheat ; clothes were no longer bought, but, again, there was no spare butter, meat, milk, or cheese for sale. Besides, the farmer could not expend more than his capital in wages, and his capital, far from being increased by this new mode of cultivation, diminished gradually. A great part was converted into fixed capital, in the shape of buildings, machines, and utensils without number, which were necessary in order to carry on such various occupations. The result was that the supply of labour was the same, but the means of paying for it diminished, and a fall in wages ensued.

This is a representation of what happens to a nation which isolates itself by retaliatory duties. It multiplies the branches of its industry, I allow, but it diminishes their importance. It adopts a more complicated distribution of industry, but not a more profitable one ; for the same capital and the same amount of labour must be employed to overcome more natural obstacles. Its fixed capital absorbs a great portion of its circulating capital—that is, of the funds which should be appropriated to the payment of wages. That part which remains circulating is parcelled out in vain, for it does not augment the mass. It is as if we believed that the waters of a lake became more abundant because, when distributed into a multitude of reservoirs, they touched the ground in more points, and presented a larger surface to the sun, forgetting that this is precisely the cause why they are absorbed, evaporated, and lost.

A certain amount of capital and labour being given, they will create a quantity of produce so much the less in proportion to the number of obstacles to be overcome. So international restrictions, forcing in each country capital and labour to overcome more difficulties of climate and temperature, will result in less produce being created, or, what comes to the same thing, fewer gratifications being afforded to society. Now, if there is a general diminution of gratifications, how can the share of workmen be increased?

[I cannot omit to notice that the Fair Trade manifesto seeks authority for retaliatory duties from the following words of Adam Smith :—"It *may** sometimes be a matter of deliberation how far it is proper to continue the free importation of certain foreign goods when some foreign nations restrain by high duties the importation of some of our manufactures into their country. *Revenge in*† this case naturally dictates retaliation, and that we should impose like duties upon some or all of their manufactures coming into our country." The sense in which Adam Smith uses the word " dictates " in this passage is not that of " command," but of " suggestion." We might read the word " suggests " in its place without forcing the meaning he intended his words to bear. This is evident from what follows, for Adam Smith proceeds to give several instances of unsuccessful retaliation, adding—" There may be good policy in retaliations of this kind when there is a probability that they will procure the repeal of the high duty complained of. When there is no probability that any such repeal can be procured, it seems a bad method of compensating the injury done to certain classes of our people to do another injury to ourselves. Every such law imposes a real tax upon the whole community, not in favour of that particular class of workmen who are injured by our neighbours' high duties, but of *some other class.*" Book IV., c. 2. Yet this halting opinion in favour of retaliation,

---

* " Must " in manifesto.
† " Revenge in " omitted in manifesto.

pronounced, be it remembered, more than one hundred years ago—when political economy was in its infancy—is to be now made our rule of conduct and our guide.

The following illustration of Dr. Franklin's shows how retaliatory duties might affect this country :—

England has, say, three manufactures—silks, iron, woollens—and supplies three other countries—Germany, France, Belgium. The silk trade is suffering somewhat, and England wishes to increase the sale, and raise the price of silks in favour of her own silk workers.

In order to do this she puts a duty upon French silks.

France, in return, raises her duties upon English iron.

Then the iron-workers complain of a decay of trade.

And England, to content them, puts a duty upon iron castings coming from Belgium.

Belgium, in return, levies an increased duty upon English woollens.

Then the woollen-workers complain of decay.

And England levies a duty on woollens coming from Germany.

Germany, in return, levies increased duties upon silk goods coming from England.

What is got by all these retaliatory duties?

Answer :—All four countries find their common stock of enjoyments and conveniences of life diminished.]

CHAPTER XII.

THEORY AND PRACTICE.

"You may flatter yourselves that your free-importation system is right," say the Fair Traders; "but for our part we believe in the *old experience* and sagacity of the other European countries."

What do we say, and what do you say?

We say :—

"It is better to buy from others what would cost us more to make for ourselves."

And what do you say?

"It is better to make things for ourselves, even when it

would cost us less to buy them from others, for it employs labour."

But, gentlemen, putting aside theory, demonstration, and reasoning—all of which you declare yourselves nauseated with—which of these two assertions is supported by *universal practice?*

Go into the fields, workshops, factories, and warehouses ; look above, beneath, around you ; examine the operations in your household ; observe your own constantly repeated acts ; and say, what principle governs the acts of labourers, workmen, contractors, and shopkeepers ? What is your own personal practice ?

Does the farmer make his own clothes? Does the tailor grow his own corn? Do you make household bread when you can buy it cheaper of the baker ? Do you put down your pen to use the blacking brush, so as not to pay *tribute* to the shoeblack ? Does not all social economy depend upon the separation of occupation, upon the division of labour—in short, upon *exchange?* And what is exchange but the result of a calculation which we all make, and which leads us to believe that if we discontinue direct production, and obtain things indirectly, we shall save both time and trouble ?

You are not then *practical men,* for you cannot point out a single man on the surface of the globe who acts in accordance with your principles.

But you say, " We have never intended to make our principles the rule of *individual* conduct. To do so would be to force men to live like snails, each in his own shell. We limit ourselves to the assertion that our principle should govern the relations established between agglomerations of the human family—between nations."

Well, this is still erroneous. The family, the parish, the municipality, the county, are so many agglomerations which all, without exception, *practically* reject your principle, and have never even thought of it. All procure by means of exchange that which would cost them dearer to obtain by means of production. Nations would do the same thing if you did not prevent them by force.

It is we, then, who are the practical men—the men of experience.

Our theory is so little opposed to practice that it is merely *practice expounded.* We observe the actions of men, impelled by the instinct of preservation and of progress, and their free and voluntary acts are what we call *political economy*, or the economy of society.   We repeat, unceasingly, every man is *practically* a good political economist, producing or exchanging, as he may find it most advantageous to produce or to exchange. Each by experience arrives at the science, or rather the science is only this same experience scrupulously observed and methodically expounded.

But you make a theory in the bad sense of the term.   You conceive and invent modes of acting, which are not sanctioned by the practice of any living man, and then you would call restriction and prohibition to your assistance.

I defy you to apply to international concerns a doctrine which you confess is absurd when applied to the transactions which take place between individuals, families, parishes, towns or counties.   By your *own* avowal, it is only applicable to international concerns ; and this is the reason why you are obliged to repeat at every turn :—

"There are no such things as absolute principles.   That which is *good* for an individual, a family, a parish, a town, a county, is *bad* for a nation.   That which is *good* in detail—for instance, to buy instead of producing, when buying is more advantageous than producing—even that is *bad* for the body politic ; the political economy of individuals is not that of nations," and other extravagant assertions of the same sort.

And why is all that ?   Examine it closely.   It is to prove to us that we, as Consumers, are your property ; that we belong to you ; that you have an exclusive right over us ; that you may feed and clothe us at your own prices, whatever may be your unskilfulness, or your inferior capacity.   No, you are not the practical men, you are the men of unverified theories,— theories which lead you, wittingly or unwittingly, to spoliation.

CHAPTER XIII.

RECIPROCITY AGAIN.

"ARE we sure that the foreigner will purchase from us as much as he sells to us ? " say the Fair Traders.

[Mr. Ecroyd does not doubt about it for one moment. He is quite certain that the foreigner will not.   He says—" The nations from whom we chiefly purchase our supply of food, and who, until the past five or six years, took large quantities of our manufactures in payment, will now take them from us no longer.   They have shut out our goods by heavy duties. Thus the English workman's employment, by which he earned the money to pay for his imported food, is taken from him!"] *

I admire the manner in which men who, above all things, call themselves *practical*, reason contrary to all practice!

In practice, can there be any bargain to the amount of a hundred, a thousand, or ten thousand pounds, which is a direct barter of produce against produce?   Since money has been introduced into the world, has any man said, "I will not buy my shoes, hats, advice, lessons, of any shoe-maker, hat-maker, lawyer, or master, who will not buy my wheat for an equivalent value?"   And why should *nations* impose such a restraint upon themselves?

How do such things come about?

Suppose a nation deprived of all foreign intercourse.   A man has grown some wheat; he puts it into the *national* circulation at the highest rate which he can get for it, and receives in exchange—what? sovereigns; that is to say, orders for goods, infinitely divisible, by means of which he can withdraw from the national circulation at his own convenience, and at its just value, whatever he may want or wish for.   Definitively, at the end of the operation, he will have withdrawn from the mass precisely the equivalent of that which he has put in; and in value, *his consumption will have exactly equalled his production.*

As exchanges between this country and others are free, it is not into *national* circulation, but into *general* circulation, that every one puts his productions and takes out from it what he consumes.   It does not signify to a man whether what he puts into general circulation is bought by a fellow-countryman or a foreigner; whether the goods which he receives come from an Englishman or a Frenchman—whether the articles against which he exchanges the goods which are necessary to his wants have been made on this or that side of the English Channel.   There will always be an exact balance between what he puts in and what he takes out of the great

* *Burnley Advertiser* (letter to), Sept. 15th, 1879.

common reservoir; and if this is true in the case of an individual, it is true, also, with regard to the whole nation.

The only difference between the two cases is, that in the last instance each has access to a more extensive market in which to make his sales and purchases, and consequently has a better chance of making them both on advantageous terms.

This objection has been made : " If every one is agreed not to take out of circulation the produce of a certain individual, he on his side could take nothing out of the mass.   This would be the same with regard to a nation."

The answer is this :—If this nation could withdraw nothing from the mass, it would put nothing into it ; it would work for itself; it would be obliged to submit to that to which you would beforehand subject it—viz., *to be isolated.*

[Now let us apply this argument to England, and first let us hear what Sir E. Sullivan says :—"Will foreign nations buy more of *our* goods if we put a duty on *their* goods ? Certainly not.   They will continue to buy from us just what they do now, neither more nor less, but we shall buy £40,000,000 to £50,000,000 less of their goods."   How can this be possible ? We know that we are not paying for foreign produce with precious metals—nor with foreign bonds (p. 40).   It is there- fore certain that whatever we take from foreign countries we pay for in produce.   How on earth then are foreign nations to pay us for the goods they take from us if we do not take theirs in exchange?   The statement of Sir E. Sullivan is simply absurd.

But the idea underlying these words of Sir E. Sullivan is— that by buying of the foreigner we are depriving the English labourer of employment.   This idea pervades the Fair Traders' arguments.   Their manifesto, quoting the words of a foreign Protectionist, M. Pouyer Quertier, says :—"We want the English consumer to accustom himself to the use of the products of French industries ; we do not want our consumers to accustom themselves to use British commodities ; "—" and so," compla- cently adds the manifesto, " say most other foreign statesmen." Sir E. Sullivan and " most other foreign statesmen " are, there- fore, completely in accord.   The fallacy that the purchase of foreign produce deprives our countrymen of labour has been lucidly exposed by Mr. Porter, in the following illustration :—

" Will any one tell me," said a noble lord, " that when he buys and wears a pair of French boots, he does not encourage

French labour at the expense of his own countrymen, whom he deprives of employment?" One would really think that the fallacy involved in this question is too transparent to deceive any one. Let us trace the operation. M. Lecocq, of Paris, sends to London a pair of boots, in the making of which have been employed French tanners, curriers, and boot-makers. The boots are sold in London, and paid for in coined money. This coin does not find its way to Paris, but M. Lecocq draws a bill upon his London agent, and for this bill he obtains five-franc pieces from a Paris banker, who sells the bill to an ironmonger having to pay a London merchant for metal sent to him from this country. The bill, at maturity, is discharged from the money paid by the buyer of the boots— M. Lecocq having paid the leather merchant and his workmen with the money he received from the Paris banker. It is not, of course, pretended that this is the precise course pursued; but a course equivalent to it is followed in ninety-nine cases out a hundred. Let us, however, suppose what, according to the noble lord's position, is the very worst that can happen— viz., that M. Lecocq receives the identical coin given in payment for his boots. This no further alters the operation than by complicating it in some slight degree. Whence has the coin been obtained? England has no mines of gold, and must purchase the precious metal which it needs with its iron, its coals, its cotton, linen and woollen manufactures; and having need of more gold by reason of the payment made to M. Lecocq, will send a piece of linen to California in order to purchase it. "Will any one tell me that in buying and wearing M. Lecocq's boots I have not given employment to the miner and smelter in the first case, or to the linen-weaver in the second case?"

The Fair Traders treat with the most unmitigated contempt the principle that the more we buy from foreigners the more they must buy from us; yet there is nothing more absolutely certain. To diminish our purchases from them, by the imposition of retaliatory duties, would compel them to lessen their purchases from us. The purchase of the French boots enabled the Paris smith to pay for the English metal. English labour was employed just as much as before, only it took another form.

Now, does any Free Trader propose that we should not adopt the electric light because its adoption would displace the labour of gas-men and others, or was it ever suggested that we should orego the use of railways because they would throw a number of coachmen and post-boys out of employment? If purchasers seek what they require abroad, it is because the articles they need are produced there with greater economy—the money sent to pay for them will certainly return to the English workman to pay him for the goods sent abroad as the equivalent for our purchases. Labour will be employed just as much as before, and the community, as the consumer, will be benefited by the difference in cost.

When we commenced to take off the duties on foreign goods, although foreign countries made no corresponding reductions, and in some instances nearly doubled and trebled some of their duties as a defensive measure, they were, nevertheless, compelled in the course of a very few years to double and treble their purchases from this country. As we purchased more freely of them, they had to take our goods in return.

But then comes in the juggle of money, and people fail to see that even if we send bullion to pay for our purchases we must export our labour in some form to obtain the bullion, so that it comes to exactly the same thing as if we exported our own produce immediately in return for our foreign purchases.]

Money is simply a medium. John has completed a coat, for which he wishes to receive a little bread, some meat, a visit from the doctor, a ticket for the play, &c. The exchange cannot be effected in kind, so what does John do? He first exchanges his coat for some money, which is called *sale*, then he exchanges this money again for things which he wants, which is called *purchase*, and only now has the reciprocity of services completed its circuit. It is only then that the exchange is complete.

[Retaliatory duties can only result in loss to the consumer. If, in spite of their imposition, we still continue to purchase of the foreign producer as before, the whole of the increased cost of the article purchased will fall upon the consumer, and be to him a dead loss (*e.g.*, the husbandman, p. 44). If, instead of purchasing from the foreigner, we transfer our custom to the home producer, the consumer will still be a loser to the extent of the increased amount he has to pay to obtain from the home producer an article equal in quality to that he formerly obtained from the foreigner. If this was generally understood, many, who now hanker after retaliatory duties, would cease to do so.

TRADE AND FOREIGN DUTIES.

Many occupations undoubtedly feel the effect of foreign duties severely. The fishermen of Yarmouth and the east coast bitterly resent the heavy duty which France levies upon "bloaters." They are more than half-disposed, in consequence, to approve of retaliatory duties. What would be the effect? Lessened purchases by us, and, as a consequence, lessened purchases by France. Who can say, if John ceased purchasing French silks of Louis, for his wife, that Louis would be able to continue purchasing Yarmouth bloaters for the consumption of his family on fast days. He now can pay for his bloaters with his silks, but if we no longer take his silks in payment, he will have to cease buying bloaters in return.

Sometimes there escapes from the lips of Free Traders expressions such as : " I should not object to seeing import duties placed upon luxuries." Of course such expressions can only come from those who have not thoroughly mastered Free Trade principles. The illustration I have just given is sufficient to show this. Silks, velvets, &c., are always classed under luxuries, and yet we see that the purchase of silk may enable a large number of men to be employed in herring fishing—not an occupation supported by a love of luxury—who otherwise might have to lay aside their fishing, and turn their industry to the production of the silks, &c. which we should be hindered by duties from importing.

Unfortunately there are few things which suffer more from an unjust stigma than so-called luxuries. The term "luxuries," truly understood, indicates not any particular class of produce, but rather the wasteful abuse of any kind of produce in ways inconsistent with sobriety.

Whether we call duties imposed upon foreign produce by the name of " Protective " duties, or of " retaliatory " duties, their effect upon consumers and upon the prosperity of the country will be identical. The following table is interesting as showing what Protective duties have been doing for the colony of Victoria during the past ten years. (See *Daily News*, Aug. 16, 1881.)

Population of Victoria, census of 1871	731,000
Returns of excess of births over deaths from 1871 to 1881	146,000
Number of immigrants registered as arriving to settle in the colony from 1871 to 1881 ...	53,000
Total	930,000
Number of actual population, census 1881 ...	855,000

The conclusion to be drawn from these figures is that between 1871 and 1881 no less than 75,000 persons—more by 22,000 than the number of her immigrants during that period—found the fiscal system of Victoria so unfavourable to their well-being, that they left the country and emigrated to places offering fewer impediments to prosperity.

According to an interesting parliamentary paper just published by the Board of Trade, the reports of eighty-five Chambers of Commerce in Germany denounce with remarkable unanimity the new Protective tariff in that country. They say that it " has restricted trade, and at the same time enormously enhanced the cost of living, thus materially deteriorating the condition of the people." Wages are lower in Germany than in England, but owing to the Protectionist tariff the prices of many necessaries of life are higher there than with us—Bacon and cheese stand at double our prices, bread 20 per cent. higher, sugar, tea, coffee, rice, &c., all dearer. House rent also is higher. They have to exercise a " constant careful pinching, of which we have no idea in England." The working man " rarely tastes butcher's meat ; " he has "to live on watery soup ; fuel, too, is frightfully dear."

Does any one ask what would be *our* condition under a system of " Protection " or " retaliation," whichever we are pleased to call it, for the result would be the same?

Let him turn back to the tales of the dark days of Protection in the '30's and early '40's—to Dickens's " Old Curiosity Shop," for instance, and little Nell and her grandfather frightened by the bread-rioters in the iron-blast districts of Birmingham. Then we were in much the same condition as Germany now. Sugar cost three times as much as it does now. Tea was five shillings a pound ; coffee half-a-crown. Bread fluctuated enormously in price. There was no cheap, wholesome jam for the little children. There was little schooling ; the average duration of life was less ; the death rate was higher. There was no prospect but of a hard struggle for bare subsistence from the cradle to the grave. The people were worse housed, and the Protective tariff, instead of raising, kept down the rate of wages. Misery and discontent were rife throughout the land.]

CHAPTER XIV.

"NO SUCH THINGS AS FIXED PRINCIPLES."

NOTHING is more astonishing than the way in which men resign themselves to ignorance about things which are of the utmost importance for them to understand. And when we hear men give utterance to this axiom :—"There are no such things as fixed principles," we may be quite sure that they have no real wish to dispel their own ignorance.

One man says : "If you continue to tolerate this one-sided Free Trade, the foreigner will inundate you with his productions—the American with wheat, the Frenchman with sugar, the Spaniard with wool, the Italian with velvet, the Belgian with cattle—so that there will remain no field for native industry."

Another answers, "If you forbid these exchanges, all the various benefits which nature has bestowed upon each climate will be for you as if they had no existence. You would gain nothing from the fecundity of the American soil, from the fertility of the French, from the cheapness of Spanish labour, from the warmth of the Italian climate, nor from the richness of the Belgian pastures, and you would be obliged to obtain, by a forced production, that which by exchange you might procure as a natural produce."

Assuredly one of these is mistaken. But which one? It would be worth while to inquire, for this is not a mere question of difference of opinion. Two roads are before you ; you must take your choice, and one of them necessarily leads to *misery*. In order to escape the difficulty, you say, "There are no such things as fixed principles."

But if exchanges have not a natural law of their own, either of exclusion or of freedom, if they are capriciously useful or mischievous, if, in short, there are no fixed principles, then we must ponder over, balance, and regulate transactions ; we must equalise the conditions of labour ; an Herculean task, well fitted to secure to those to whom it is intrusted large salaries and great influence.

On entering London, one might reflect, "There are 4,000,000 human beings here who would die in the space of a few days if there were not a constant influx of all kinds of provisions

E

to this vast metropolis." Imagination takes fright at the task of enumerating the immense multiplicity of articles which must pass into that vast city to-morrow, without which the lives of its inhabitants might fall a sacrifice to the convulsions of famine, riots, or pillage. And yet all are now sleeping, without a thought of so dreadful a prospect to disturb their peaceful slumbers. On the other hand, all the counties of England have been labouring all day, without mutual agreement, in order to supply London. How does it happen that every day an exact supply is brought to this gigantic market? What, then, is the intelligent and secret power which presides over the astonishing regularity of such complicated operations ; a regularity in which all have such thoughtless confidence, although their welfare and lives depend upon it? This power is a fixed, *an absolute principle*, the principle of the freedom of trade. We have confidence in that impulse which Providence has placed in the hearts of all men to whom it has confided the preservation and indefinite amelioration of our species—in *interest*, since we must call it by its right name, which is so active, vigilant, and provident, when it has freedom of action. What would be your condition, Londoners, if a minister thought fit to substitute for this power combinations made by his genius, however wise he might be? Suppose he should think fit to take the entire direction of this prodigious machinery, and to hold all its springs in his own hands, to determine by whom, where, how, and on what conditions each article should be produced, transported, exchanged, and con- sumed? Although there is much suffering within your precincts, although misery, despair, and perhaps starvation, may cause more tears to fall than your zealous charity can dry, it is pro- bable, nay, I will say it is certain, that the arbitrary intervention of Government would infinitely multiply those sufferings, and would bring upon all the evils which now affect but a small number of your fellow-citizens.

Now, having this confidence in a principle when it acts upon our home affairs, why should we not have equal confidence in the same principle acting upon international transactions, which are certainly no less numerous, no less delicate, and no less complicated? And if it be not necessary that a Minister of Commerce should regulate our branches of industry, should weigh our chances, our profits, and our losses, should be occupied with the distribution of our currency, and should equalise the conditions of labour in our internal trade, why should it be necessary that the Custom House officer, going beyond his fiscal province, should pretend to exercise a protecting care over our foreign commerce.

[But to return to the question of the existence of "fixed principles," one of the Fair Trade arguments in favour of retaliatory duties is, "Yes, we quite admit the principles of Free Trade, but then you know that there are exceptions to every rule." There may be exceptions to every rule, but there are no exceptions to principles. The real drift of the assertion is that "there are no such things as fixed principles."

But permit me to point out that there can be no exceptions to the rule even of Free Trade without adopting a complete change of principles. For how can you make an exception in favour of one producer and refuse to do the same for another? If you tax American wheat to please the farmer, you must tax Belgian castings to please the iron-master. If you tax French silks to please the silk-weaver, you must tax velvets to please the velvet manufacturer. If you tax ribbons to please Coventry, you must tax woollens to please Bradford.

And what will be the result? Prices will rise all round, and upon the rise in prices will follow a diminished demand. Labour, consequently, will find less employment.

Some Fair Traders are more logical. They do not ask for " exceptions to the rule," but for a total subversal of the principles of Free Trade. Yet even some of these men are clearly to be numbered amongst those who believe that there are " no such things as fixed principles," for some who would subvert our present fiscal system have said that "Even 'one-sided' Free Trade has been beneficial to the country until within the last few years." And what is that but saying that there are no such things as fixed principles?]

CHAPTER XV.

NATIONAL INDEPENDENCE.

AMONG the arguments brought forward in favour of the retaliatory system, we must not omit that of *national independence.*

"What should we do in case of war," is said again and again, "if we depend upon foreign countries for our food?"

E 2

And the French monopolists on their side exclaim :

" What will become of France in time of war if she depends on England for her coal and iron ?"

We do not consider one thing, which is, that the sort of dependence which arises from exchanges, from commercial transactions, is a *reciprocal* dependence.   This is the only true *reciprocity*.   We cannot depend on foreigners without foreigners depending on us.   Now this is the very essence of *society*. To break the natural relations is not to place ourselves in a state of independence, but in a state of isolation.

But observe well, we isolate ourselves from the fear of war, while the mere act of isolation is the beginning of war.   It makes war more easy, less onerous, and consequently less unpopular.   If nations offered to each other permanent markets, if their intercourse could not be interrupted without bringing the double infliction of privation and embarrassment, they would no longer have occasion for those powerful fleets which ruin them, nor for those immense armies which crush them.   The peace of the world would not be compromised through the caprice of a Bismarck or a Salisbury, and war would disappear through want of incentives, resources, motives, pretexts, and popular sympathy.

I know that I shall be reproached for making interest the basis of the fraternity of nations,—vile and prosaic interest ! People would be better pleased to think that the principles of union rested on charity and love, that it even required some abnegation of self—that while injuring the material well-being of men it could claim the merit of a generous sacrifice.

We scout, we despise *interest*, that is to say, the useful and the good—for to say that all are interested in a thing is to say that this thing is in itself a good—as if interest were not the necessary, eternal, and indestructible spring to which Providence has entrusted human perfectibility.

After all, it is strange to find the sentiments of the most sublime self-denial brought forward to support spoliation itself. Here then is the end to which this fastidious disinterestedness leads.   Men so poetically delicate that they will not have peace itself if it is founded on the vile *interests* of men, would put their hands into the pockets of others, and, above all, into those of the poor ; for retaliatory duties would raise prices and lessen the demand for labour.   Gentlemen, dispose as you please of what belongs to yourselves, but give us leave also freely to dispose of the fruits of our labour—to use or to exchange them according to our wishes.

[This bugbear of our dependence upon foreigners has ever been one of the strong points urged against Free Trade. To expose the utter hollowness of this argument we have only to turn to the pages of history, and what do we find there? In 1809-10, when the power of Napoleon had reached its zenith, when his will was law throughout Europe, and when his most strenuous efforts were directed—by the Berlin decrees, which declared the British Isles to be in a state of blockade, closed all harbours against ships coming from Britain to European ports, and rendered all English goods and manufactures found in foreign territories liable to confiscation—to place England in a state of complete commercial isolation, we imported from the continent 2,000,000 quarters of grain, chiefly wheat, and of this, 1,000,000 quarters came to us direct from France, and the Netherlands—the Netherlands being then practically part of the French Empire. And this was no "one-sided" trade, for at that very moment the troops of Napoleon were marching through Europe shod with boots from Northampton, and clad in great coats from Leeds.]

To reject foreign goods and to destroy machinery are two acts which proceed from one and the same doctrine.

There are men who clap their hands when a new invention is given to the world, and who, nevertheless, would reject the produce of foreign labour. These men are very inconsistent.

What objection do they bring against our Free Trade system? That it is hurtful to *national industry*.

In like manner ought they not to object to machinery, which accomplishes by natural agents that which would otherwise be the work of our hands, and consequently injures *human labour*?

The foreign workman, placed in more advantageous circumstances than the English workman, is, with regard to the latter, a real *economic machine*, which ruins him by its competition. In like manner a machine which performs a certain operation at a lower price than it can be done by hand is, with regard to hand-labour, a true foreign competitor, which paralyses it by its rivalry.

If, then, it is advisable to protect *home industry* from the competition of *foreign industry*, it is not less advisable to protect *manual labour* from the rivalry of *mechanical labour*.

Whoever adheres to such a system, if he has any logic in his head, ought not to limit himself to prohibiting foreign productions, but should likewise proscribe the productions of the shuttle and the plough.

I have therefore more respect for the logic of those men who, when they declaim against the invasion of foreign merchandise, have the courage likewise to declaim against the *excess of production*, due to the inventive powers of the human mind.

If it is true, *a priori*, that the domain of invention and of industry can only be extended the one at the expense of the other, we ought to find fewest workmen in Lancashire, for example, where there are most machines. And if, on the contrary, we can bring forward *as a fact* that machinery and human industry co-exist in a greater degree in rich nations than in savage nations, we must necessarily conclude that the two powers are not incompatible.

I cannot understand how a thinking being can rest satisfied in the presence of this dilemma :—

Either the mechanical inventions and labour-saving appliances of man are not hurtful to his industry, as general facts attest, since there are more of them to be found among Englishmen and Frenchmen than among the Zulus and Fijians ; or else the discoveries of the mind put limits to human industry, as particular facts seem to show ; for I every day see a machine take the place of twenty or a hundred workmen. There must therefore be a direct conflict between the intellectual and physical powers of man—between his progress and his well-being ; and I am forced to declare that man ought to have had given him either his reason or his hands, his moral or his physical strength ; but that Providence, by conferring on him at the same time faculties which mutually destroy each other, has made sport of him.

The difficulty is urgent, and you escape from it by this strange apophthegm :—

There is no fixed principle in political economy.

That is to say, in plain language,—

" I do not know what is true or what is false ; I am ignorant of what constitutes the general weal or woe ; I will not give myself the trouble to find it out. The immediate effect of each measure upon my personal welfare is the only law which I consent to recognise."

There are no such things as principles! That is as if you were to say that there are no such things as facts ; for principles are only the *formulæ* which result from an order of well-attested facts.

Machinery and importations have certainly some effects. Are these effects good or bad ? We may differ in opinion on this subject ; but whichever view we may adopt, we must accept one of these *two principles :* that machinery is a benefit, or that machinery is an evil; that importations are advantageous, or that importations are injurious.

But to say *there are no such things as fixed principles,* is to descend to the lowest point of degradation of which the human mind is capable.

But you will say to me, " Destroy the fallacy. Prove to us that machinery does not injure *human industry,* nor importations *national industry."*

In a work like the present, such demonstrations cannot be very complete. My aim is rather to propose difficulties than to solve them—to incite men to reflect rather than to satisfy their enquiries. Convictions cannot be properly forced on the mind, except by its own workings. I will, however, try to lead the way.

The adversaries of importation and machinery are deceived, because they judge of them by their immediate and transitory effects, instead of following them out to their general consequences.

The first effect of an ingeniously designed machine is to render a certain amount of manual labour superfluous for the production of a given result. But its effect does not stop here. Inasmuch as the given result has been obtained with less effort, it will be offered to the public at a lower price, and the sum of the savings thus realised by all purchasers enables them to demand fresh objects of desire ; that is to say, to encourage manual labour in general, precisely to the amount which has been subtracted from the particular industry in which the improvement has been effected.

It is not that the demand for labour has lessened, but that the demand for objects of desire has increased.

Let us make these effects plain by an illustration :—

I will suppose that England consumes 10,000,000 hats, at ten shillings each. That will produce to the hat manufacturers £5,000,000. A machine is invented, by means of which hats can be sold at five shillings each. The returns of this manufacture will be reduced to £2,500,000, providing the consumption does not increase. But still the £2,500,000 will not be subtracted from the payment of *manual labour*. Saved by the buyers of hats, they will use it to satisfy their other wants, and consequently to remunerate general industry all the same. With the five shillings which he has saved, John will buy a pair of shoes, Henry a book, Edward an article of furniture, &c. Manual labour, taken in the gross, will continue to be encouraged to the amount of £5,000,000; but this sum will give the same number of hats as before, besides the advantages procured by the £2,500,000 saved by the machine. These advantages are the net profit which England will have drawn from the invention. It is a gratuitous gift, a tribute which the genius of man will have drawn from nature. We will not deny that in the course of the transformation a certain amount of labour will have been *displaced*, but we cannot admit that it will have been destroyed, or even diminished.

In like manner as to importations. Let us resume the hypothesis.

England manufactures 10,000,000 hats, which are sold at ten shillings each. The foreigner invades our market, and supplies us with hats at five shillings. I maintain that this will in nowise diminish national industry. For we must produce to the amount of £2,500,000 in order to pay the foreigner for the 10,000,000 hats at five shillings each.

And then there will still remain over the five shillings which each purchaser will have saved on his hat, the total sum of £2,500,000, which will be spent on other purchases —*i.e.* will pay for other labour.

The amount of work will remain the same, and the surplus purchases, represented by the £2,500,000 economised on the hats, will form the net profit of the importation, or of Free Trade.

[Some labour will be displaced, but quite as much labour, nay more, will be employed in the aggregate, and every consumer will be benefited. The poor, also, as the largest consumers, will be placed in the position of being able to fight the battle of life on more favourable terms than they could before. It is an exploded notion that if you import what you made before, workmen are deprived of labour. It is not so. They are employed on other work to supply the articles which are wanted to pay for the new imports.]

CHAPTER XVI.

"THE FREE IMPORTATION OF RAW MATERIALS."

IT is said the most advantageous trade is that in which manufactured articles are given in exchange for raw materials, for these raw materials afford employment for *national labour*.

Whence it is concluded :—

That the best system of customs duties would be one that gave the greatest facilities possible to the admittance of *raw materials*. The Fair Traders fully adopt this principle, and advocate absolute Free Trade in raw materials, while upon all imported foreign manufactured goods they propose to levy duties—10 per cent., says Sir E. Sullivan.

There is no fallacy in political economy more widely spread than this fallacy concerning the free importation of raw materials. Not only is this idea entertained by the Fair Trade school, but even by many Free Traders themselves, an unfortunate circumstance, for the worst that can happen to a good cause is not that it shall be strongly attacked, but that it should be weakly defended.

Prove to me that the *value* of the articles of merchandise which you propose to admit without duties—cotton, wool, skins, copper, &c.—is not due to labour, and I will agree with you that it is useless to place retaliatory duties upon them.

But, on the other hand, if I demonstrate to you that there is as much labour in £5 worth of wool as in £5 worth of cloth, you ought to acknowledge that retaliatory duties ought to be levied upon the one as much as upon the other.

Why is this sack of wool *worth* £5? Is it not because it cost £5 to produce? And is the cost of production any other thing than the sum which was distributed in wages, manual labour, interest, &c., to all the workmen and capitalists who have joined in its production?

The cotton-grower cannot pretend to have *created* the cotton, but he can pretend to have given to it its *value*—that is to say, to have transformed into cotton, by his own labour, and by that of his servants, his horses, and his gatherers, those substances which before did not at all resemble it. What does the cotton-spinner do more, who converts it into fabrics, or the draper who makes it into shirts?

In order that man may clothe himself in broad cloth a host of operations are requisite. Before the intervention of all human labour, the really primitive or *raw materials* of this production are air, water, heat, the gases, light, and the salts which enter into its composition.

Here then are the raw materials which truly are independent of all human labour, since they have no value. But a first labour converts these substances into fodder, a second into wool, a third into yarn, a fourth into cloth, a fifth into garments.

Who will venture to say that all in this work which gives exchangeable value, is not *labour*, from the first movement of the plough which begins it, to the last stitch of the needle which terminates it?

And because—to obtain more celerity and perfection in the accomplishment of the required work, a garment—the labour is divided among several classes of industry, you would make the order of succession of these labours, by a merely arbitrary distinction, the only measure of their importance, so that the first is supposed not to merit even the name of work, while the last is regarded especially as labour, and is alone deemed worthy of the favour of retaliatory duties.

The Fair Trade manifesto says truly that "it is the utility of labour which gives exchange value," but it does not explain that *all value* is due to labour. Nature assists the farmer in the material formation of grain; I will even admit that this is exclusively her work, but you must allow that the farmer has compelled her to it by his labour; and when he sells you corn you must remember that he does not make you pay for the *work of nature*, but for *his labour*.

The manufacturer is also assisted by nature? Does he not, by the aid of the steam-engine, make himself master of the expansive power of steam, while the farmer, by the help of his plough, makes use of the qualities of the soil and air? Did the manufacturer create the laws of expansion and of the transmission of forces, or the farmer the qualities of the soil and air?

Coal is certainly the work, and the exclusive work, of nature. That is certainly *untouched by any human labour*, but labour gives to it its value.

Copper, too, had no *value* during the millions of years that it remained unknown and buried underground. We are obliged to dig for it ; that is labour. We are obliged to carry it to market ; that again is labour ; and the price which you pay for it in the market is nothing else but remuneration for the labour of raising and transporting it.*

Thus the *value* of raw materials, as well as of manufactured goods, depends on the price of production, that is to say, on *labour ;* for it is impossible to conceive of any article possessing *value* which shall have been untouched by *all human labour.*

The point insisted upon by the " Fair Trader " is that it is more advantageous for a nation to import those materials denominated *raw*, whether they are the produce of labour or not, than to import manufactured articles.

" Raw materials," they say, " being the elements of labour, ought to be subject *to a different system*, and admitted *without restriction.*"

All this is based on an illusion.

We have seen that all *value* represents labour ; now, it is true that the labour of the manufacturer increases the value of raw material ten-fold or a hundred-fold, that is to say, extends the profits of the nation ten or a hundred times. Therefore we reason thus :—The production of a ton of iron only brings £2 to the labourers of all classes ; the conversion of this ton of iron into watch-springs raises their earnings to £2,000, and can one venture to say that it is not more to the interest of the nation to secure for itself labour to the amount of £2,000 than to the amount of £2 ?

We forget that international exchanges, no less than individual exchanges, are not made by weight and measure. We do not exchange a ton of raw iron for a ton of watch-springs, nor a pound of uncombed wool for a pound of wool made into cashmere, but a certain value of one of these things *for an equal value* of another. Now, to barter equal value for

---

* I do not here explicitly mention what part of this remuneration falls to the share of the contractor, the capitalist, &c., for several reasons : Firstly, because if we examine closely we shall discover that their share will always consist of reimbursements of money advanced and for previous *labour.* Secondly, because under the general term of labour I comprehend not merely the wages of the workman, but the legitimate remuneration for all co-operation in the work of production. Thirdly, above all, because the production of manufactured articles is just as much burdened with interests and remunerations, apart from those of *manual labour*, as that of raw materials, and the objection, futile in itself, would just as well apply to the most delicate fabric as to the coarsest agricultural produce.

equal value is to barter equal labour against equal labour. Therefore, it is not true that the nation which sells cashmeres and watch-springs to the value of £10 gains more than the one which sells £10 worth of wool or iron.

In a country where no law can be passed and no tax levied without the consent of those whom that law is to govern, or on whom that tax is to be imposed, the public cannot be robbed without first being deceived. Our ignorance is *the raw material* of every extortion to which we are liable to be subjected, and we may be quite sure that every fallacy is but the forerunner of robbery. I would warn the public, when they see a fallacy put forward, to put their hands on their pockets, for they are certainly about to be attacked.

If the Fair Traders were logical, they would propose to levy duties upon raw as well as upon manufactured produce ; but this would probably bring upon them the wrath of the shipping interest, for we can hardly suppose that the shipping interest would regard with complacency any proposal to levy duties on the £365,000,000 worth of raw produce which we import.

The Fair Traders, however, avoid this danger by a subtle economic distinction between raw and manufactured produce ! They would impede the importation of finished productions, but allow the more costly transport of raw materials mixed with all their dirt and refuse—this gives more employment to the shipping interest—this is a wise economy !

Why not then require that larches should be brought from Russia with their branches, their bark, and their roots ; the gold of California in its crude state ; and the skins of Buenos Ayres still attached to the bones of the decayed carcases ?

If such principles were to prevail, I expect that we should soon find the shareholders in railroads, if they had ever so small a majority in the House of Commons, passing a law forbidding the manufacture at Burton-on-Trent of pale ale to be consumed in London, in order that the transport of the grain, &c., might furnish the industry of London with *the indispensable material for labour*, and thus set to work the whole of their locomotive power.

[M. Lecocq sent us a finished manufactured product— boots (p. 61). "This," say the Fair Traders, "deprives national labour of employment. We do not object to the importation of hides from which boots are made, for they would be in the nature of raw produce, and would provide employment for our workpeople." How absurd this now seems. Hides are less valuable than boots, inasmuch as there has been less labour spent upon them. By importing hides, and not boots, we should have consequently less to pay the foreigner for the same quantity of materials. The labour of English shoemakers would be needed to manufacture the boots ; but then, as we should have imported less value, we should have to export less value in payment, and the iron-monger and other foreign buyers of our produce, unable to obtain bills for boots drawn upon us by M. Lecocq, would have to restrict their purchases from the London metal mer-chants to the amount that we might have been indebted to France for hides.

In short, the more numerous our purchases of foreign manufactured goods, the larger must be the amount of home labour employed for the foreign market, so that it *is unimportant whether we ourselves use the products of home labour, or whether we export those products to pay for the foreign products which we import.* It is similarly unimportant whether our imports take the form of raw materials or of manufactured goods, for the employment of home labour must be certainly as extensive in the one case as in the other.]

How long shall we shut our eyes to this simple truth? Industry, naval power, labour, have for their aim the general good—the public good. To create useless branches of industry, to favour superfluous transports of goods, to give employment to unnecessary labour not for the good of the public, but at the expense of the public, is the object, although not clearly perceived by him, of the "Fair Trader." Labour is not in itself a desirable thing : all labour without adequate result is a loss. If you pay sailors to carry useless refuse over the sea, you might as well pay them to play at ducks and drakes with pebbles upon the surface of the water. Thus we arrive at this conclusion, that all *economic fallacies*, in spite of their infinite variety, have this in common, that they con-found the *means* with the *end*, and develop the one at the expense of the other.

CHAPTER XVII.

METAPHORS.

" God preserve us," said Paul Louis, " from the evil spirit and from metaphors!" The sword which *malice* puts into the hands of the assailants would be powerless if fallacies did not break the shield on the arm of the assailed, and it has been well said that "*Error is the cause of human misery.*"

How are men misled on these subjects? A few words of ambiguous meaning do the mischief.

Such a word is *invasion.*

An English woollen manufacturer says, "Let us preserve ourselves from the *invasion* of French woollens." An English landlord exclaims, "Let us repel the *invasion* of American corn." And they propose to raise barriers between the nations. Barriers occasion non-intercourse; non-intercourse leads to hatred; hatred to war; war to *invasion.* " What matters it?" say they; " is it not better to be exposed to an eventual *invasion* than to agree to a certain *invasion?*" And people believe them.

Yet what analogy is there between an exchange and an *invasion?* What similitude can possibly be established between a ship of war, which comes to scourge our cities with fire and sword; and a merchant-ship, which comes and offers to barter freely, voluntarily, foreign productions for ours?

I shall say the same of the word *inundation*—" Flooding our markets," says Sir H. Giffard.* This is taken ordinarily in a bad sense, because it is the general characteristic of inundations to lay waste. If, however, they leave upon the soil a value superior to that which they take away, like the inundations of the Nile, we should be grateful for them, if we did not, after the example of the Egyptians, bless them and deify them. Before, then, declaiming against *inundations* of foreign products as flooding our markets, before placing in their way troublesome and costly obstacles, we should ask if they are among those inundations which lay waste, or those which fertilise? What should we think of the Khedive, if instead of construct-

* Launceston, Oct. 27th, 1881. *Western Morning News.*

ing dams across the Nile, in order to extend the region of its *inundation*, he were to expend his piastres in deepening its bed, in order that Egypt might not be contaminated by the *foreign* slime brought down from the Mountains of the Moon? We exhibit precisely this degree of wisdom and of reason when we wish, by the expenditure of millions, to preserve ourselves——from what? From sharing the advantages with which nature has endowed other countries.

A celebrated modern philosopher has added to the categories of Aristotle a fallacy which consists in comprising, in one word, a begging of the question. He quotes various examples of it. He might have added the words *invasion* and *inundation*, in an economical sense, for certainly they both take the question for granted.

Such a use of words conveys utterly false ideas to the mind. You might as well say that it is the same to *give* £10 perforce to one who has his hand at your throat, as to *give* it willingly to one who in return supplies you with the object of your wishes. You might as well say that it is a matter of indifference whether you throw your bread into the river or eat it, because in either case the bread is *consumed*. The vice of such reasoning consists in accepting a complete similitude between two cases by reason of certain points of resemblance, while taking no account of their points of difference.

CASSELL, PETTER, GALPIN & CO., BELLE SAUVAGE WORKS, LONDON, E.C.

www.ingramcontent.com/pod-product-compliance
Lightning Source LLC
Chambersburg PA
CBHW020336090426
42735CB00009B/1563